The Supercharged Teen

The Potential of a Young Life

Rick Gerber

ISBN-13: 9780692204511
ISBN-10: 0692204512

Acknowledgements

THE SUPERCHARGED TEEN was written as a result of my desire to challenge young people. I fully recognize that I am not alone in this desire, for many men and women have devoted their lives to youth ministry and counseling. It is to these individuals that I offer a big thumbs-up, for without their influence, the lives of many a teen may never have been changed for the better.

I also wish to share that my hands were not the only ones to prepare this book; for a number of helpful and busy friends gave of their time and effort into what would become the final product. To those who took the time to read the manuscript – Peter, Josiah, and Aaron, I'm so thankful for your input. A special thanks to Jerry and Pastor Clyde for their very valuable insight and critique. To Betty, who was willing to edit my poor grammar and actually make the book readable, I thank you. I also desire to express my appreciation and deep respect for Olivia, Ryan and Sarah; the three *Supercharged Teens* who allowed me to share their stories in the last chapter. You each stand as examples before your peers as individuals who not only desire to use your God-given gifts and abilities, but are in the very process of committing your lives to that end. I trust that each of you will prove to be a blessing to many.

Thank you likewise to my precious wife and children for your patience, as I spent many hours at the computer developing this book into a reality. I love each of you very much.

Above all, I wish to thank and praise my Lord Jesus, without whom I would be and could do nothing.

Contents

Introduction

EVERYWHERE I GO, I witness young people of the teenage years conforming to the standards and expectations of those around them. Being so unique as individuals, their own personalities and characteristics are frequently denied the chance to express themselves. My heart goes out to those who conceal or ignore their God-given gifts and abilities in an effort to be accepted into their sphere of friends. As a parent of four children, two of whom are teenaged, one pre-teen, and one post-teen, and having served alongside my wife as youth leader within our church, I am burdened to write this book to any young person who is willing to be challenged. Up front I would like to make it very clear that I've received no formal theological training, I've secured no degree in psychology or counseling, nor can I lay claim to any formal education past high-school. What I do have, however, is what I believe to be truly vital, for what I do have is a genuine concern for the young people of this generation. Along with that is an unwavering burden to challenge every teenaged guy and girl to utilize his/her massive potential as an individual. I fully recognize that there are many excellent books available that are written with our youth in mind. This book is in no way superior to any other, nor is it my intention to provide any new, groundbreaking insights into the subject of youth motivation. On the other hand, I would prefer this not be read as a book, but as a conversation between me and you, as a young person. I have a genuine desire to challenge and encourage teens just like you. Therefore, all I ask of you as a young person reading this book is to lend me your ears and your heart; and, if you are willing to apply what you are about to read, you will leave this "conversation" with a mindset that, with your God-given gifts and abilities, the fulfillment of your dreams and goals is well within your reach.

Supercharge yourself!

1

Supercharged... or Not!

AS I TURN back the clock over 30 years, I can still recall the excitement of me and my like-minded teenage buddies driving our musclecars, whose combined horsepower contained more focused energy than a freight train on steroids... or so it felt. I recognize that times have changed, and the musclecars of yesteryear have been replaced by an entirely new breed. The purpose is the same, however, to provide the driver with a thrill that lasts a lifetime. The excitement of a powerful engine has never changed, and that's where the purpose of supercharging becomes reality. For those who may not understand the supercharger's function, please allow me to clarify. A supercharger is nothing more than a system which forces air into the interior of an engine. More air means more oxygen. More oxygen means more fuel is burned, resulting in an increase of power.

As I look back on time, the supercharged engines of those who could afford such extremes were the standouts on the Saturday night "circuit," as we would call the approximate six mile loop through town. Ah, yes... supercharged. The very word promotes goose bumps the size of marbles. Supercharged, in the recesses of my feeble mind, means but one thing...

To be charged with an overabundant or excessive amount of energy, drive, determination, and purpose.

In the context of a tire-smoking supercar, the word seems most fitting; however, I see absolutely no reason at all why the very same goose-bump-the-size-of-a-marble producing word cannot be applied to the human being... especially those like you – the living, breathing, modern teenager! My greatest concern, as I see and carefully observe so many youth, is that there is a huge degree of contentment living life with little or no intention or purpose in mind. Now, at this point you may be thinking, "What gives this pre-modern, antiquated teenage wanabee the right to judge us?" I shall answer that logical question in this way.

~Conformity~

I've seen it time and time again. Teenagers unknowingly define who they are, based upon the influences of those around them. Strange as it is, I find particular enjoyment sitting or standing in a public place simply watching young people – teens shopping, walking, talking, and basically just interacting with those around them. Even though each individual has his or her own personality, his or her own physical, emotional, intellectual, and spiritual "uniqueness," time and time again I am forced to ask myself the same questions. "If they are all so different in these many, many ways, why are they so much alike? Why is it that so many, of not only our teenagers, but adults as well, fit so well into the mold of mediocrity? Why is it that there seems to be such a uniform mindset?" "What mindset?" you might ask. "What mold of mediocrity?" Allow me to explain. Unless I am terribly mistaken, it certainly appears obvious that most individuals with whom I come in contact, even on a casual basis, young or old, have the tendency to display one or more of the following attributes:

- a reluctance to pursue their dreams and/or goals,
- a fear of failure,
- a lack of self-confidence,
- a habit of complaining,
- a sense of discouragement,
- an air of frustration,
- a feeling of discontentment.

So why is it that so many teens, as well as adults, as living, breathing individuals, with different personalities, convictions, goals, etc., all seem to display so many of the same emotional characteristics? As I ponder this mystery, I believe I can confidently give one reason that is overwhelmingly obvious. We are all influenced by those around us. We are influenced by our families, friends, fellow students, co-workers, the media, and the list goes on.

If you don't agree with me, I issue this one simple challenge. The next time you find yourself in a public place; whether it is a church or an amusement park – the location doesn't matter – take notice. You don't need to be a brain surgeon to recognize that individuals, especially of the teenage years, who are hanging out, have the uncanny ability to speak the same, act the same, and display the same types of attitudes and habits, almost as though they are a unique subspecies unto themselves. And, furthermore, as you consider the sight before you, the important question is... are these individuals displaying a "supercharged" nature, or are they displaying the subdued, laid back and downright "normal" nature that is characteristic of much of society? Clones they appear to be; however, clones they are not. As a teen, only you can decide whether or not, or to what degree, you will display yourself as you really are... for the whole world to see. In all of your uniqueness, whether you are a guy or a girl, please recognize that there are always two sides of a coin. And the coin of your life can either be flipped to supercharged or non-supercharged. I hope to be able to turn on the stadium lights of your imagination, as we consider together the decision that you, and you alone, must make as a young person.

To conform or not to conform... that is the question. Though this book is written with the Christian teenager in mind, the truths and challenges contained within apply without a shadow of a doubt to every young person. If you are alive and breathing and are able to read the words written here, I challenge you to take them to heart.

~Be Unique~

So what does it mean to be unique? Within the context of this book, allow me to share what uniqueness is NOT. Uniqueness is NOT the act of dressing, speaking, walking, or displaying a character that purposefully draws attention to yourself. Like birds performing their courtship rituals, too many individuals are attempting to be total standouts, or should I say, "stand-alones," crying out to the world around them, "Here I am... look at me!"

Could it be that, as eye-catching as that person may be, he or she is accomplishing nothing more than a puppet's fulfilling the demands of the puppeteer of personal insecurity? Proving of little benefit to himself or the culture in which he lives, his actions likely mask the potential within, the potential of the supercharger that lies within each human being.

You may ask yourself the question, "What is it that makes me so unique?" This is an excellent question that is easily answered with a bit of thought and reflection. As I reflect on my own personality and my own interests, I need not think long to recognize those interests, abilities, and personal preferences that, in and of themselves, define who I am. They define the types of individuals around whom I feel most comfortable. They also influence the activities in which I spend my time. Allow me to take a moment to reflect upon some of my own inborn characteristics that, when combined, define who I am. Ever since childhood I have had a deep fascination with nature, particularly reptiles. Along with that, I prefer to be alone, I do not like dressing up in overly nice clothes, and I detest the taste of coffee.

I've likewise been gifted with artistic skills, as well as an ability to speak comfortably before a large group of people.

Now you may be thinking to yourself that these are ridiculously vague and shallow personal characteristics, and, in a way, you are correct in your thoughts. But the point I'm trying to emphasize is that these, when combined with many other personal characteristics, serve to define who I am as an individual. They combine to give me the potential to become the person that my Creator wants me to be. You and I are unique, and, because we are unique, we are special. And because we are special, we have tremendous value, not only in the eyes of God, but also to those around us. We will be considering our value in the next chapter, so I will not dwell on it now.

I would challenge you to reflect upon yourself. What are those things that have been with you all of your life? Your convictions, your interests, your beliefs? An interest in sports, table games, or other social activities? Or perhaps even a love for children, or a compassion for the elderly? Write them down, reflect upon them, and then ask yourself this question...

Am I willing to allow these characteristics to freely define who I am and the decisions that I make from day to day?

If your answer to this question is yes, then you are well on your way to firing up the supercharger within.

If, on the other hand, you find yourself suppressing these personal characteristics in an effort to conform to or be accepted by your friends, then the question must be asked of yourself...

Am I always going to allow myself to conform to the standards or the convictions of those around me, rather than being the unique, special person that God has created me to be?

As long as you are living and breathing, you have the capability within to accomplish so much of what most people would view as impossible. Standing firm on your own convictions, beliefs, and characteristics and allowing them to define and determine your every decision and motivation, you will be able to live what I am referring to in this book as a supercharged life – a life with which you can influence one person or millions of those around you.

In December, 1955, on the first day of the month, an African-American woman of 42 years was riding a Montgomery city bus on her way home from a busy day working as a seamstress. Seated in the mid-section of the bus, she and three other blacks suddenly found themselves being ordered by the driver to give up their seats. Due to the then existing laws of racial segregation, the whites had seating privileges over the blacks. Thus, as the bus filled, she and three other blacks were required to stand, allowing the whites to take their place in seating. As the three other black individuals relinquished their seats, Mrs. Rosa Parks refused, resulting in her being arrested for violating the laws of segregation and subsequently ushering in a new era in America, an era of racial equality.

Had Rosa Parks gone along with the crowd, had she failed to act upon her own beliefs and convictions, the sprouting era of civil rights may not have taken the sudden leap as happened at that time.

Many individuals, youth as well as adults, fail to realize their full capabilities because they allow themselves to fit snugly into the mold of mediocrity that shapes so many within their realm of influence. As a youth, there may be things you want to do and ways you may want to better yourself, but you find yourself captive to this same mold of mediocrity – a mediocrity that is holding you back, a mediocrity that is being prompted and encouraged by those in your crowd.

As you take a good look at yourself, your personality, your interests, and your goals, ask yourself the question…

What would I look like, how would I talk, what would I be doing, if I didn't care what people thought of me? Would I dress the same, speak the same, act the same? Would I be more driven to achieve my dreams and goals? Would I be more likely to live out my own personal convictions?

Please understand, I am in no way implying that being yourself, turning the other way regardless of what others may think, just being the person God made you to be is easy! In reality, it takes a tremendous amount of courage to be you – to be different, allowing your own passions, interests, and motivations to surface! It takes courage, an inner strength that is beyond that which is normal – a strength and courage that, once allowed to surface, can profoundly influence the rest of your life and the lives of those around you.

As a young person, consider this...

Are there people in your life – your friends or the crowd with whom you spend time – who are hindering you from fully expressing yourself, your values, your purpose, and your personal goals?

If we find ourselves involved in relationships with those who encourage us to engage in any activity that will, without a doubt, physically, emotionally, or spiritually harm us in any way, it is definitely to our benefit to face the facts and, as hard as it may be, take appropriate steps to lessen their negative influence in our lives, even if that requires severing the relationship. Far too many young people (as well as adults) willfully ignore this simple truth and suffer the consequences of it. However, along with these obviously harmful relationships, there are also relationships that, though not directly threatening as described above, are likely to lead us into a lifestyle which threatens to rob us of the desire to fulfill our dreams, our passions, and our convictions. It is on that very context which I am trying to place my emphasis here. It is very important to realize that, if you hang around with nine non-driven, lazy, unmotivated people, you WILL become number ten! I hope I'm making sense to you. Life is too short to allow others to influence YOUR degree of motivation and YOUR goal setting and achieving. Feel free to maintain these friendships; however, the application of wisdom and discernment is vitally important in keeping yourself and your dreams on track and intact. Keep this one thing in mind: if **you** don't program your mind, others will!

~It's All about Attitude~

There is another negative influence we regularly face, both from the outside and within. Since I'm moving along like a jet-fighter with a tailwind, I will now progress into the area of grumbling and complaining. Allow me to begin this section with the admittance of my own pitiful failure in this area. Yes, I am a grumbler and complainer. There are many things that downright irritate me, and I often find great fulfillment in expressing my irritations to others. This is a destructive habit that I myself am in the process of overcoming. Because of this struggle in my life, I feel quite comfortable to address the issue in the lives of others. We all know people around us who appear to make it their goal in life to find fault with all that life has to offer. If we give them an apple, it's not red enough... if we give them a compliment, they question our motives. These are the type of people who are single-handedly destroying their chances of ever being able to live a life of fulfillment and contentment. As a young person you need to recognize that life will have its disappointments. Life on a daily basis will give any human being plenty of reasons to complain and plenty of events about which to complain. The problem with complaining is that it's just like a dream. You can spend all night dreaming that you're working at a task, but, when you wake up, you've accomplished nothing. So it is with complaining. I so frequently see it in action with my children. I will ask them to perform a simple ten-minute task, and they spend eleven minutes complaining and telling me why they don't want to do it, all the while not realizing that, had they not been complaining, the task could long ago have been completed. So it is with you and me. We all need to look this pitiful attitude straight in the eyes and with great determination proclaim boldly and confidently that it will control us no longer. Sometimes we take life's bumps and bruises much too seriously. We must learn to recognize those "irritations" in life that are truly worth taking seriously and, likewise, those at which we simply smile and walk away. I regularly witness people complaining about the most ridiculous things, irritated at even the simplest inconvenience. When I was a pre-teen, an older couple in my neighborhood defended their lawn as though their lives depended on it. Day by day, as my friends and I would walk by on the sidewalk in front of the neighbor's home, we could sense their observant eyes burning holes through us – watching, waiting, and expecting us to willfully and defiantly take even one step onto the perfectly manicured lawn. Oh, what a sorrowful waste of their time and energies. As a youth, you need to expect the unexpected from life, deal with life's frustrations, and learn to handle them.

"Life is like an onion: You peel it off one layer at a time, and sometimes you weep."

Carl Sandburg

Life is going to slap you around; it slaps everyone around. When you're least expecting it, when you feel comfortable and confident... you get blindsided! So we whine and feel sorry for ourselves. We gripe and complain about how unfair life is to us. I do want you to please take note of this one simple truth: when you gripe and complain, most of the people who hear really don't care, while the rest are happy it's you, and not they. The very act of complaining is nothing more than a waste of your precious time and energy, for it accomplishes absolutely nothing resulting to your benefit.

Every day of your life serves as a building block that will consistently shape you and form you into the person you will ultimately become. Every day serves as a foundation for developing character, personality, achievement, and attitude. Depending upon how you let each day shape you, you will be either developing or deteriorating in these areas. How we handle life's daily struggles and victories determines what shape our lives will take.

A negative attitude is a destructive attitude. Studies focusing on the relationship between attitude and health indicate a definite connection between positive attitude and good health. With a positive attitude our minds will experience a greater freedom in creativity, goal setting, and the ability to turn life's lemons into sweet lemonade. And that will then be one positive step in cranking up the supercharger within!

In finishing up this first chapter, let's carefully reflect upon some major points we've just considered.

Think about it...

- **Supercharged is to be charged with an overabundant or excessive amount of energy, drive, determination, and purpose.**

- **Every individual has his or her own personality, being unique physically, emotionally, intellectually, and spiritually.**

- **So many teenagers, as well as adults, define who they are, based upon the influences of those around them.**

- **In conforming to the expectations of those around you, you fail to allow yourself the realization of your full potential as an individual.**

- **Life will have its disappointments. Every day serves as a building block that will shape and form you into the person you will ultimately become. How you handle life's daily struggles will ultimately determine the shape your life will take.**

2

The Value of YOU

WITH THE PREVIOUS chapter I emphasized the fact that those around you have a considerable amount of influence upon your character, motives, ideals, goals, etc. Unfortunately, the views you have of yourself are likewise frequently determined by the comments and actions of those with whom you come in contact. Words are powerful. The spoken or even the implied word can radically change how you think of and view yourself. How many times did you experience a crushed spirit as the result of another person's words concerning your looks, your character, or even your personality? Regardless of what other people may say about you, you must not lose sight of your true value – your value not only in the eyes of God, but also your value to your friends, your family, and the world in which you live. You were created to be unique for a reason. In being unique, you hold value. If there were vast numbers of diamonds, all alike in their quality, their value would be much less. However, because quality diamonds are rare, their value increases. So it is with all young people, different as they are. But, oh... you are much more valuable than the most costly diamond, for even the most costly diamond cannot influence the world as can you, a young person. As you begin to grasp your tremendous worth as a human being, especially as a teen, still another step will be taken toward enabling yourself to realize your full God-given potential, and, in that, you will be one step closer to experiencing a super-charged life.

~Created for a Purpose~

Let's reflect a moment upon **Psalm 139, verses 13 and 14**, wherein you can gain a deeper insight into your actual creation as an individual.

"For you created my inmost being; you knit me together in my mother's womb. I praise you because I am fearfully and wonderfully made ..."

It is difficult to read this portion of scripture without being reminded that you have a purpose. The very fact that you were made should tell you without doubt that you exist for a purpose. I say that because obviously nothing is made without a reason for its being made. Allow me to clarify in a most simplistic way. Cars are made so we don't need to walk everywhere we go. Jackets are made to keep us warm in winter. Lightbulbs are made so that we can see when it would otherwise be dark. Contact lenses are made so that, when we're hot and sweaty, we can see without glasses which tend to slide down our nose. "Those are ridiculous examples," you might say. Right you are… but you certainly get the point, I hope. Again, nothing is made without a reason for its existence. You were made; therefore you have a purpose. And, if you have a purpose, you also have value.

The references to being "knit together" and "fearfully and wonderfully made" are clear indications that your Creator applied thought, emotion, and care into the process of designing you. God, and God alone, possesses the sovereign skill and abilities to successfully create you in all of your complexity, your beauty, and your purpose. I am not a scientist, but all one needs to do is spend a bit of time researching life at the molecular level to fully understand the complexity of it all. Some molecular biologists spend their entire careers engaging only in the study of individual functions of the cell. How special you must be, made with such precision and care.

As a parent of four children, I am at a loss to tell you how many times my children would spend time crafting, cutting, pasting, and assembling something special in their own eyes, after which they would joyfully present this beautiful creation to my wife and me. To witness the sheer delight and fulfillment which was so obvious by the smiles on their faces made it very clear that they were proud of their achievement. And we can only imagine this same joy, this same delight and fulfillment at the time of our creation – a creation brought forth at the hands of an all-powerful, all-knowing God, who loves us, and created us for a purpose.

~See Yourself for Who You Are~

Do you find yourself frequently admiring the achievements of others? Are you drawn to other individuals who take "center stage" and are honored as the result of something special they have accomplished? Do you lie awake at night (or daydream during the day) visualizing yourself as the focal point of others' attention, putting yourself in their position of glory? How often we elevate others, rather than accepting our own special position in life. We "put down" our own qualities which make us so very valuable, in favor of dwelling upon what others have or what others can do. Every person is special. Every person is valuable. Each individual is truly endowed with a unique set of personal attributes which make him/her precious in his/her own way. I am not saying that you strut around as proud as a peacock, viewing yourself as more special than everyone else. I would like to emphasize, however, that you, too, are special. You have absolutely no reason to view yourself as inferior to anyone else. Far too many times I've heard others bluntly putting themselves down with comments like "I wish I'd be that attractive," or "Man, I would love to be that strong." How many times has someone complimented you, and you found yourself rejecting their complement? Someone may comment, "I like the way you have your hair today," to which you rashly respond, "It looks ok, I guess... I spent an hour getting it to this point." Why not just say, "Thank you," and accept the compliment given you? Again, I'm not promoting pride or arrogance. Rather, I'm encouraging you to take an honest look at yourself and accept the fact that God made you and He made you right. He endowed you with a personality that only belongs to you. As a side note, I'd like to share something that is truly mind-boggling to me. Our emphasis has been on the reality that we were created and that we were created for a purpose.

I've always found it incredible that we have not only been so carefully created, but that our Creator loves us. He loves us so much that He sent His Son, Jesus Christ, to pay our debt as sinners. If not for His Son Jesus, indeed, we would have no hope, no life. Only in personally trusting Jesus, accepting His sacrifice on the cross, can we enjoy this true hope and life, both now and into eternity. I say "personally" trusting Jesus, because it's a decision that every person must make. We are all sinners, and it's only through Christ's sacrifice on the cross that we can receive forgiveness and have any real hope. The Bible clearly emphasizes these truths.

"...for all have sinned and fall short of the glory of God..." Romans 3:23

"Salvation is found in no one else, for there is no other name under heaven given to men by which we must be saved." Acts 4:12

"Yet to all who received him, to those who believed in his name, he gave the right to become children of God..." John 1:12

"That if you confess with your mouth, 'Jesus is Lord,' and believe in your heart that God raised him from the dead, you will be saved. For it is with your heart that you believe and are justified, and it is with your mouth that you confess and are saved."
Romans 10:9, 10

Furthermore, as children of God, we will always remain firm in the grasp of His love.
Consider **Romans 8:38, 39.**

"For I am convinced that neither death nor life, neither angels nor demons, neither the present nor the future, nor any powers, neither height nor depth, nor anything else in all creation, will be able to separate us from the love of God that is in Christ Jesus our Lord."

Allow yourself to ponder this truth. Your Creator loves you, and in Christ nothing can change this fact. If that doesn't make you feel special, absolutely nothing will. You are a child of the King, a member of the royal family. Knowing this, you have absolutely no reason to lack confidence in yourself, because your abilities and attributes are God-given. You need to recognize your own gifts and abilities for what they are and seek to further develop them. So often the only difference between you and somebody whom you admire is the fact that you hold back those God-given abilities, while they allow those abilities to be fully expressed in their lives. Whether it be the gift of music, creativity, or athletic prowess, it makes no difference at all. You have value. You have skills. You have inborn attributes that, when exercised, can be honed and developed to a high level of perfection. Consider professional athletes, artists, musicians, speakers, or writers. Each one of those individuals made a personal decision to exercise his gifts, develop his gifts, and expose his gifts for the whole world to view, to enjoy, and from which to benefit. In reality, that is the very reason we look at those people and have the tendency to elevate them above ourselves. They hold no greater value than that of you. They merely allow that value to express itself, while you and I keep it tightly bound within us, never allowing it to see the light of day. Again, I am not insisting that we elevate ourselves above others. To develop the mindset that we are somehow better than everyone else is not only wrong, but it is pure arrogance. You're not better than anyone else... but... you're not less than anyone else, either!

If you feel inferior to others, it's nobody's fault but your own. As Eleanor Roosevelt said, "No one can make you feel inferior without your consent."

~Confidence~

As I mentioned previously, I enjoy watching people. And as I watch and observe, it's pretty easy to recognize individuals who display an air of confidence and those who do not, simply by the way they walk, talk, and interact with others. I previously referred to the follower of Christ as being a member of the royal family. As a member of God's family, there is no reason why you should not show confidence through the way that you present yourself while being around others. When speaking with someone, look him/her in the eyes, which reveal a sense of boldness, courage, and resolve. Maintaining visual contact during a conversation conveys to that person that you believe in what you are telling him, that what you have to say is important. Also, as you maintain eye contact with him, you will be ensuring him that what he has to say is likewise worthwhile and valuable. On the other hand, communicating with someone while looking down at the floor immediately sends a message of weakness, distraction, or lack of concern. The spoken word is powerful. However, the word spoken while making eye contact can make a huge difference in whether or not the person accepts you and what you have to say.

The way you carry yourself from day to day is an indication of how you view yourself, whether or not you have a personal respect and confidence. This confidence will send a very clear message to others that you are a young person with potential, an individual who knows what he or she wants and has plans to achieve it.

Self confidence, or the lack of it can be a significant influence on how you handle and ultimately react to the peer pressures around you. Ask yourself these questions:

Do I feel defeated when my peers point out my physical "flaws"?

Do I make an attempt to "fix" these flaws – for example, change my hair style or perhaps dress differently to conceal my physical flaws (as pointed out by my peers)?

Do I try to make excuses for saying or doing something of which my peers may have disapproved?

Do I hesitate to express my spiritual beliefs or convictions for fear of how my peers may react?

Do I fail to share my dreams and my goals with those in my group because of a potential negative response from them?

~Pressured by Peers~

The list of questions could go on. Consider carefully the answers to these questions. If you find yourself answering yes to one or more of them, ask yourself why. Why do I choose to react in a manner that would please my peers, rather than please myself or my God? Am I concerned about rejection? Do I fear being ridiculed and mocked? Do I simply want to "fit in" with my group, being accepted by them?

As a teen, I can recall many moments when I was forced to feel less than adequate as a human being. It hurts to be ridiculed and degraded before a group of friends. It hurts to experience the rejection of those close to you who you trust and count on for support and encouragement. In my early teens I was regularly picked on because I lacked significant "stature." In other words, I was short and skinny. I was determined to overcome the ridicule, so I began working out with weights. I started out with two or three days of training a week. Within a year or two I was recognizing an increase in strength and size, as my workouts took on a greater degree of intensity and frequency. By the time I graduated from high school I was bench pressing nearly twice my body weight. I was still short, but to a great degree I was realizing a self-confidence that I had not experienced before. So why do I share all this? Looking back, in a very real sense I caved in to the pressures around me by taking steps to change the way I appeared to my peers. I feel that this was a poor choice on my part, because, as I said, I gave in to peer pressure. I experienced an unwillingness to accept myself the way I was. On the other hand, in a positive sense, I not only took steps to overcome my adversity, but I likewise became engaged in an activity that would benefit me health-wise long into the future. To this day I work out on a regular basis and very much enjoy the health benefits thereof.

If you find yourself giving in to pressures within your group, consider thoughtfully the potential harm in doing so. The decisions you make now can and will influence the rest of your life. Keep in mind that as an adult you may look back with deep regret at the decisions you made as a youth. I am keenly aware of too many adults who live with such regrets. You may be asking, "So how do I deal with the peer pressures that I face?" Allow me to share what I feel in this regard. The questions you must ask yourself are twofold.

What are the specific pressures that I face most frequently?

What are the potential negative consequences of my giving in?

~Wisdom Is Priceless~

Giving in to some pressures may have no significant consequences, while others (drugs, alcohol, sex, etc.) have the potential to be absolutely disastrous. In these difficult situations you must choose not to give in. Rather, share your situation with adults whom you trust, whether they are parents, family members, pastors, or youth leaders. As difficult as it may be to accept, very often the adults around you may lend tremendous advice and guidance. The insight that a wise adult can provide may have a huge influence on your life. Please take note that I used the word "wise." According to the Scriptures, wisdom holds value above all else that we can imagine.

"Blessed is the man who finds wisdom, the man who gains understanding, for she is more profitable than silver and yields better returns than gold. She is more precious than rubies; nothing you desire can compare with her." Proverbs 3:13-15

Without a doubt, wisdom is priceless, for it guides the young and old alike in every area of their lives. It preserves, protects, and leads those who seek it and hold onto it. So what in the world is wisdom? Wisdom is simply the ability to judge or to discern the difference between truth and error, between that which is right or wrong, beneficial or non-beneficial. It is to see and understand the events and activities taking place around us in all circumstances. Simpler yet, it is the proper application of knowledge. Humans are not born possessing wisdom. Wisdom must be sought after and learned. Indeed, true wisdom ultimately comes from God.

"If any of you lacks wisdom, he should ask God, who gives generously to all without finding fault, and it will be given to him." James 1:5

The reason so many older individuals display wisdom is due to the fact that many of them have "been there and done that," and have allowed the many lessons they have learned throughout life to shape and develop a discerning mind. Likewise, you as a young person need to seek wisdom for all its worth, striving to gain a spirit of discretion and understanding that will serve to guide, preserve, and keep you through all the decisions you will need to make. This same wisdom will then enable you to stand firm in the midst of temptation and peer pressure, as you will have gained a deeper understanding and recognition of those pressures and how to deal with them in a manner that will preserve you as an individual.

In closing this chapter, I again need to emphasize the fact that you are precious in the eyes of your Creator. You are precious in that you were created for a purpose. And in having purpose, you hold great value. In Christ you have the privilege of being a child of the King. There will always be those who seek to steal your "crown." However, crown or no crown, you still hold value — value to yourself, and value to the people around you.

Think about it...

- The very fact that you were created indicates that you have a purpose.

- You have value because you were created for a purpose.

- The way you walk, talk, and interact with others shows that you have confidence in yourself and the abilities that God has given you.

- When struggling with peer pressure, seek the help of others who can guide and encourage you in making right decisions.

3

It's Your Life... What Are You Going to Do with It?

AS I HAD mentioned at the end of the previous chapter, you, as a created individual, are indeed precious. The life that God has given you and me is without doubt precious above all else. Just like all other created things, whether the home you live in or the shoes on your feet, you, too, will one day wear out and expire. A brand new sports car or a newly purchased outfit, as beautiful as they are when new, have a limited period of time in which they are useful. To put it plainly, everything has a limited life-span.

"Time is free, but it's priceless. You can't own it, but you can use it. You can't keep it, but you can spend it. Once you've lost it, you can never get it back."

Harvey Mackay

As we take this into consideration, we must realize that each day of our lives, each hour of the day, and each minute of the hour holds a tremendous amount of value and potential. As a young person, you have considerable advantages over those who are more advanced in years. Think about it a moment; you have physical strength, energy, and a mind that is capable of being shaped, formed, and sculpted like putty. You also have your whole life ahead of you, which means more time to develop yourself in order to achieve your dreams and goals. Ask yourself these simple but critical questions:

How do I spend my time on any given day?

Are my daily activities at all geared toward bettering myself in any way?

Am I on a regular basis engaged in those things which will develop me physically, intellectually, emotionally, and spiritually?

~Time Is Precious~

All too frequently we take our time for granted, as though it will run on forever. If there is anything that frustrates and annoys me, anything that irritates me more than my son's stinky feet, it's when I hear somebody make the statement that they are just "killing time."

As far as I'm concerned, killing time should be a federal offence, punishable by hanging the offender upside down while exposing him to five years of non-stop opera. Time and time again I see people, young and old alike, just hanging out, while gazing intently, almost in a hypnotic state, into the screen of a miniature hand-held device. I've seen my own kids, focused to the point of never blinking, never acknowledging my presence, totally oblivious to their surroundings, sucked in to the realm of whatever that miniature form of technology has to offer. At this point you may be experiencing a good bit of disdain toward me as a result of my expressing my opinion of this matter. For this I do not apologize, for I believe that time is much too precious to be wasted. Before I move on with this topic, let me make it perfectly clear that we all need periods of rest and relaxation. We all, as human beings, need to take time to rest our bodies and our minds. Some people enjoy going for a walk, bicycling, knitting, watching television, or, yes, playing video games. I am not busting on the activity itself, but I am concerned with the amount of time given to those activities. If you enjoy your small electronic devices, that is absolutely wonderful if, indeed, it is a source of refreshment and relaxation for you. If you enjoy it and it's legal and moral, go for it! However, one must always consider the tendency of any enjoyable activity to become habitual in nature. Almost anything can mutate into a monster that can consume our minds, our energies, and, indeed, our very well-being as humans. This monster has a massive appetite, and the only thing that we can feed it is our time... our precious time. I beg you to dwell on this for a while, as it can make or break your ability to experience a supercharged life, a life of purpose and achievement.

If you don't want to accomplish your goals, if you don't want to fulfill your dreams, all you need to do with your time is nothing... absolutely nothing. As a result, nothing will come to pass. You will eventually look back on life and draw the conclusion that nothing invested results in nothing returned. Ben Franklin was right when he said, "Lost time is never found again." In order to experience the fulfillment of any dream or any goal, you need to invest in yourself; you need to wisely invest your time and efforts in activities that will guide you to achieving those goals, experiencing the reality of fulfilled dreams. Every individual who is successful in business, music, art, family, or even in spiritual matters has spent countless hours planning, preparing and engaging himself or herself in those areas which served to carry that person to success. Success in anything does not come without a cost. If success were easy, there would be many wealthier, more powerful, and more athletically fit people. Everywhere we look we would see master musicians, actors, artists, and the list goes on. The very fact that we tend to elevate and exalt those we perceive to be successful should be an indicator that success, as we define it, is hard to come by. Consider **Psalm 39:4, 5**

"Show me, O LORD, my life's end and the number of my days; let me know how fleeting is my life. You have made my days a mere handbreadth; the span of my years is as nothing before you. Each man's life is but a breath."

We have no idea of the length of our time here on Earth. The phrase "here today and gone tomorrow" is based on reality when applied to our lives. We can experience strength, health, and vigor one day, only to find ourselves facing tremendous physical challenges the very next.

I know of a 23-year-old man who faced this very reality. A classic example of health, muscle, strength, and speed, the very last thing on this young man's mind was to be facing the uncertainty of ever again engaging in the physical activities that he so loved. Crawling into bed at the end of a long, active summer day, he never anticipated the rapid turn of events that was to take place within the next few hours. Midway through the night he woke, not on the bed he had so recently laid upon, but upon the floor by that bed. Confused and physically exhausted, he was forced to face the reality that he had experienced a seizure, which was later found to be the result of a golf-ball sized brain tumor. Facing the possibility of a malignant tumor was the least of his concerns just hours before. Life at that moment stood still, as he pondered the uncertainty of enjoying any more of what life had to offer. Could this be it? Was he going to die at a young age? Was he never going to experience the joy of being a father? Who was going to take care of his young wife? What about his many unfulfilled dreams and goals? Many such soul searching questions pervaded his sleepy thoughts as he lay in the back of the ambulance en route to the hospital. Weeks later, following surgery, he found himself experiencing a peace, joy, and thankfulness that was beyond expression, as he came to realize that the now removed tumor was indeed benign and no longer a threat to his young life. I can boldly attest to the young man's experience, for I was that young man. I write this with tears of thankfulness, as I recall these events which took place 25 years ago.

~*Personal Development*~

I shared this experience with you to impress upon you the reality that life can be full of surprises. This fact should prompt you to take advantage of every moment, to develop yourself in areas that will be of benefit to your future.

At this point, you may be wondering how you would begin the process of self-growth, or personal development. By self-growth, I am referring to engaging in those activities which, with your goals in mind, will move you forward toward reaching those goals. If you have no specific goals at this time, why not consider setting one or more. Think about those things that get you excited, those activities in which you see others excelling and that you find yourself wishing that you would be able to do as well. Think of your future. Consider what you will be doing in five, ten, or fifteen years. Once you have a goal, whether it be short-term or long-term, set time aside each day developing yourself in areas that will make that goal a reality. Discipline yourself to use and manage your time in a profitable manner. This is time spent well, because this is time used for the bettering of yourself.

In closing this brief chapter, once again I want to encourage you to give some serious thought to how it is you will use your time from this day forward. Stay focused and determined to excel in whatever you put your mind to. Discipline yourself day by day in the proper management of each waking hour. Finally, keep in mind what someone else has so wisely observed...

"One thing you can't recycle is wasted time."
Unknown

Think about it...

- **Everything that was created has a limited life-span.**

- **Each day of your life, each hour of your day, and each minute of that hour holds a tremendous amount of value and potential for you to achieve your goals.**

- **Your time is much too precious to be wasted by just "killing time."**

- **In the process of striving to achieve goals, you need likewise to take time to rest your body and your mind simply by doing those things that you find enjoyable and relaxing.**

- **Experiencing the fulfillment of any dream or goal means investing in yourself; you need to wisely invest your time and efforts in activities that will guide you to achieving those goals.**

4

Strength Within... and Without!

IN CHAPTER ONE I encouraged you to accept yourself for who you are, who God made you to be, regardless of what others may think or say about you. We also considered that you may be content to settle into the mold of mediocrity, strongly influenced by your friends through their example in doing just that. At this point I would like to piggyback on the theme of that first chapter; however, I would like to focus more on the strengths with which your Creator has endowed you, strengths and resources that exist both within you and around you.

~Use Your Inborn Gifts and Abilities~

Every person has the capability to achieve. Goals can be set and goals can be achieved. The gifts and abilities with which you were born, combined with the abilities that you acquire and develop through personal effort, are those tools by which you will be able to achieve. These are tools that, when diligently applied, will serve to construct the framework of success in your life. Tools are of no use to the builder unless the builder chooses to pick them up and start using them for their intended purpose. A hammer will drive no nails unless carefully aimed and swung by the craftsmen who owns it. So it is with your inner abilities. You may be musically or artistically inclined, or you may have natural physical or intellectual capabilities. Many young people have the gifts of communication, hospitality, or compassion. Unless you as an individual make a purposeful decision to take advantage of your God-given natural abilities, these abilities will simply remain "on the shelf," much like an unused hammer.

You, and only you, hold the key to unlock the capabilities that the Creator has given you. If you believe in your own abilities, others will be more likely to believe in you as well, leading to even more and greater opportunities in life.

One of the biggest mistakes that you or anyone else can make is to tell yourself, "I can't do that." When we tell ourselves that we cannot do something, we usually prove ourselves right. We allow our negative attitudes to run wild, imagining loads of reasons why that "something" cannot be accomplished, and in the process we talk ourselves out of doing the very thing we want so very much to do. It has been said that the richest, most valuable place on earth is the cemetery, where lie countless inventions that were never invented, creations that were never created, and ideas that were never acted upon... from generation to generation. Don't be like so many who take their goals and aspirations to the grave with them!

So what is it that is holding you back from identifying your strengths and setting up a plan to use those strengths to accomplish your goals and dreams? I believe there are four major areas that tend to hinder most people from realizing their full potential:

- *Fear of success,*
- *Fear of failure,*
- *Contentment with "the way things are,"*
- *Squandering (wasting) time on non-productive activities.*

Let's briefly consider each one.

~Fear of Success~

It seems rather odd to mention the fear of success as a hindrance to achieving success. Upon further consideration, however, it's really quite natural for many individuals to look at the potential of success with a degree of apprehension. Success will likely bring change, sometimes radical change, which can involve both financial and personal risk. There will likely be changes to one's lifestyle, forcing a person to extend himself, perhaps physically or emotionally, beyond his comfort zone. It could involve establishing new personal relationships at the expense of existing relationships. Success frequently involves the relocation of one's self or one's family. There are changes of responsibility, both personal and job-related. Indeed, these all are sources of potential stress in an individual's life, and quite naturally one seeks to avoid that which causes stress. In seeking success, assuming you are not familiar with it, you are seeking to move into the unknown. By carefully visualizing and anticipating the potential outcomes of success, many of these fears or apprehensions can be overcome. Think about where the achievement of any particular goal may lead. If you have intentions of being a professional musician, for example, you will likely find yourself traveling throughout the country or perhaps even the world, as you perform before various audiences. It's important to anticipate these changes in life-style, even changes in culture, that you may be encountering as you move from place to place. Visualize yourself facing these changes and challenges in preparation for the real thing. You need not fear the future to the point at which that very fear has a crippling effect on your goal-reaching decisions. Yes, the uncertainty of what the future may hold can be a bit unnerving; however, with proper planning and visualization, goal-setting can be an exciting experience.

~Fear of Failure~

The fear of not accomplishing one's goals can have an absolutely devastating effect on a person's decision whether or not to establish those goals in the first place. You may have heard that tiny voice within telling you that you will certainly fail if you attempt to do this or that. How many times have you considered taking on a difficult task, only to talk yourself out of it before beginning? How many New Year's resolutions are simply never made because of past failures at achieving them? How many personal physical, financial, or spiritual goals were never set, because of that powerful little voice within that says, "Forget it... you've tried this before and failed... it's no use!"? One personal goal I've met consistently over the last 25 years or so is reading my Bible through each year. I am not mentioning this to make myself look good, for I have failed in many other areas; I'm merely bringing it up because I have known people throughout the years who have failed to reach this yearly goal, simply because they had previously tried and failed and now have the mindset that they will never be able to accomplish it. Past failures do not have power over future successes. Past failures exert no more influence over you than what you allow, so it's best to forget them and move on in anticipation of what the future can hold. You cannot allow yourself to be conditioned by past frustrations and failures. Consider an adult elephant which, being absolutely massive in weight and power, can be restrained simply by a shackle on one leg, chained to a small stake imbedded into the ground. How can this possibly be the case, when an adult African elephant can weigh an incredible fourteen to fifteen thousand pounds? The answer is simple – conditioning. It has been said that some trained elephants, when very young, have been secured to a stake in the ground by a shackle and a short chain. When young, this is sufficient to cause a degree of discomfort and restraint as the elephant pulls in an effort to move away. After a period of experiencing ongoing discomfort and restraint, the young elephant soon decides, or is conditioned, to give up all hope of freedom. Eventually growing into a huge adult with incredible strength and capability, the elephant, because of his conditioning, merely assumes that any effort to pull away would be both futile and uncomfortable.

Allowing past failures and discouragements to hinder your efforts at achieving your goals and dreams is no different than this elephant's behavior. You may convince yourself that you cannot do something, all the while overlooking the fact that the power to excel is there, just waiting for you to use it. Don't fall into the trap of telling yourself, "This is the way I am – and there's nothing I can do about it," for you will simply be erecting personal boundaries which, once set up, will be difficult to overcome. If you are going to tell yourself anything, tell yourself that, if it's physically possible, it can indeed be done. I mention "physically possible," because there are certain limitations that cannot be overcome. It irritates me when I hear people say, "You can do anything if you put your mind to it." I am 48 years old and 5'5" tall. I can tell myself until I'm blue in the face that I will one day be recognized as the MVP of a Superbowl winning football team playing the position of a lineman. The stark reality is, if I were to step one foot on that field attempting to play that position, I would be a dead man. No amount of "positive thinking" would change that; I would still be a beaten and bruised MVP wannabe. That is quite naturally the brutal truth of certain physical limitations. The problem is, however, that we impose personal limitations on ourselves that are in reality non-existent.

Don't Limit Yourself

We tell ourselves that we are not smart enough, not strong enough, or not bold enough. We insist that, if we would only have more time, money, or physical or emotional strength, we would then be able to realize our desires and goals. What we really need to face up to is the fact that many of today's most successful individuals, in reality, are no smarter, stronger, or bolder than you or I. The truth is that they have channeled the gifts and abilities they do have, combined them with a positive, winning mindset, and proven to themselves and others that they can and will make things happen in their lives. What you choose to do with your gifts and abilities will determine the path of your life.

The choices made in life can be likened to the steering of a sailboat. Though the winds of life are so often blowing against you, it is still you who has control of the rudder; thus, you can steer to determine the direction your life will take, through the decisions you make. It must be mentioned, however, that the decisions you make will be influenced by the way you look at what life offers on a daily basis. How do you view the world around you? How does your mind interpret the events that are taking place from day to day? Do you view the world as a place that is broken, challenging, hopeless, or selfish? Or do you view the world as a well-oiled, smooth-running machine that is filled with opportunity? Do you interpret the people around you as being selfish and unforgiving or as having the potential for giving support and encouragement?

At this point, you may be asking yourself what all this has to do with a fear of failure. What I am trying to emphasize is that the fear of failure can be lessened or strengthened by our attitudes, and our attitudes can be influenced by how we allow the events around us to affect our thinking. I love and appreciate what the late Zig Ziglar has said concerning the power of our thoughts.

"Positive thinking won't let you do anything, but it will let you do everything, better than negative thinking will."

An Attitude of Victory

How often do we accept defeat in our own lives before we even step into the ring. A boxer cannot win a match if he fails to make the commitment to step into the ring in the first place. Furthermore, he cannot win that match unless he commits himself to winning. He needs to have the mindset of winning, never allowing himself to entertain the thought of losing. A classic example of this kind of winning attitude was displayed on April 6, 1893, in a boxing match between Andy Bowen and Jack Burke. Meeting together in New Orleans to engage in a boxing match that may well be the longest in history, the two men battled it out for an unbelievable 111 rounds spanning a brutal 7 hours and 19 minutes. What drove each man on was nothing less than an unquenchable desire to win. Had either of the two allowed any negative attitude to take over their thoughts, the fight wouldn't have proven nearly as competitive. If you want to experience success in achieving your goals, if you long to gain a victory over some area of your life, you have to maintain an attitude that says, "I will not fail."

You can wish for something all you like, but just "wishing" will not get you the victory. You need to believe. Believe in yourself, and believe in the God-given abilities that you possess. Sure, you've made mistakes in the past. You've failed in the past. You've experienced defeat in the past. These defeats and failures can be of huge benefit to you now. Allow your past to be a school. Let it teach you the mistakes you've made, the things that went wrong, and the things that didn't work. Don't allow the past to be a burden to carry, something that will hinder your progress in the future. Don't allow past failures and struggles to beat you up time and time again. I know that you've experienced past victories. We've all experienced victories, both large and small. God regularly grants the strength, hope, and will to overcome and be victorious in any area of our lives. You need to recall, dwell upon, and gain continued strength through those victories, remembering God's enablement in the past.

Overcoming the Impossible

Many are familiar with the Biblical account of David's victory over Goliath. The event is given to us in 1 Samuel, chapter 17. At that time, when the Israelites were at war with the Philistines, the two armies found themselves in a valley facing each other. Repeatedly, over a forty day period a massive and powerful Philistine warrior named Goliath boldly and arrogantly confronted the Israelite army, challenging them to send a warrior of their own to fight him. His repeated offenses against the Israelites were relentless and fearsome. Goliath, defined as being over nine feet tall, struck terror into the heart of every soldier in the opposing army, even that of Saul, their king. One day David, who we are told was only a youth, was visiting the front lines when Goliath came forward as usual, verbally degrading the Israelites. Upon hearing the giant's arrogant and belittling words directed not only to the Israelite army, but also to their God, David became enraged. Despite King Saul's attempt to stop him, David insisted that he will be the one not only to confront the giant, but also to kill him, thus putting an end to Goliath's boastful and prideful words against Israel and their God. Armed with only a few stones and a sling to launch them, David boldly confronted the huge soldier. There were absolutely no questions in his mind about whether or not the victory would be his. There was no hesitation, no trying to talk himself out of it, no excuses as to why he may fail to succeed in his task. His mind was made up; that oversized, arrogant blowhard was coming down!

At this point we need to stop and reflect a moment and ask ourselves the questions, ***"Why WASN'T David afraid? Why was he so confident?"*** He was literally facing a nine-foot-tall killing machine who was fully armor-clad, heavily armed, and trained for war. Realistically, David was staring death in the face. But, again we must ask why David was so confident. Why no fear or apprehension? The answer is really quite obvious from Scripture. When King Saul was trying to talk David out of fighting the giant, David made it very clear to the king how his God had faithfully and powerfully delivered and enabled him in the past. David so vividly recalled God's previous faithfulness and provision in his life, that he now found himself absolutely certain that nothing in the present could stop him. He recognized that he was fully equipped for this or any task, because he was enabled by God. And his confidence in his God-given strengths and abilities did not prove false, for David realized a tremendous victory that day, as he single-handedly conquered a giant who, prior to that time, had appeared to be absolutely unbeatable. In defeating the giant, the God in whom David trusted once again proved Himself to be faithful and powerful. So in response to this amazing account of overcoming the "impossible," allow me to ask you this one question:

After reflecting upon your past personal victories, large or small, whether overcoming temptations, meeting specific goals, successfully accomplishing given tasks, or any other achievement, why would you ever doubt your God-given ability to fulfill any other goal or dream that you would seek to achieve?

You MUST answer this question for yourself, for in the answer to this question lies the reality that to doubt your potential is to cripple your potential. To doubt your potential can and will promote a mindset of failure and defeat which may hinder your accomplishments throughout your entire life, preventing any chances of your experiencing the incredible feeling of meaningful personal fulfillment.

This is the only life you have, choose to use it to its fullest potential. To fear failure is the same as choosing to fail, because in fearing failure an attempt to succeed may never be made. I like the words of Les Brown when he says, "Leap, and grow your wings on the way down." So often we fear the unknown consequences of our decisions for personal growth. There are times when you will quite simply need to GO FOR IT and then learn and develop as you move forward in life.

~Contentment with "the Way Things Are"~

As we consider contentment, I would initially like to make a clarification. In the book of *1 Timothy, chapter 6*, we read in verse 6 that *"Godliness with contentment is great gain."* I believe that, in the context of this passage, the word *contentment* is referring to a degree of self-satisfaction and the peace that accompanies it. The Greek word for *contentment* here actually implies a sense of sufficiency or satisfaction. As I share with you concerning contentment in the context of our discussion, I am certainly not promoting a desire for "more." An individual can destroy his/her very life striving for more money, more possessions, more power, or more fame as a result of greed and unthankfulness. Conversely, it is a tremendous blessing for a person to find great peace and joy in all that has been given him by God, and, in this context, I am not encouraging discontentment by any means.

When I talk about contentment with "the way things are," I am referring to a lax and unmotivated spirit that holds an individual back from his/her use of natural gifts and abilities; gifts and abilities that can bring great joy and fulfillment not only into one's own life, but also into the lives of many other people. To be a blessing and help to others should be a primary goal in the mind of every person, including yourself. I believe that anyone who wants to realize his full potential in life needs to overcome the natural human tendency to be "comfortable" or even downright lazy. It is quite obvious that nobody wants to be uncomfortable. No one purposefully seeks any thing or any activity that will in any way add stress or emotional pressures to his life. This is certainly understandable; however, you must also recognize that even as a child experiences growing pains resulting from the process of physical growth, so you will likely experience a degree of emotional pain or frustration in the process of personal growth. This cannot be allowed to quench your desire to go all out with the natural abilities that you possess.

Far too many youth and adults alike are "content" with doing nothing. Following a day at school, work, or even play, many people simply switch to a mode of physical, emotional, intellectual, and spiritual "rest" that prevents them from even thinking about pursuing anything more. This takes me right back to chapter 3, wherein we discussed the issue of how you spend your time. Again, please understand that I definitely see the need to rest. Everybody needs to rest his/her mind and body, for the human body not only demands rest, but also benefits considerably from it. A well-rested individual is like a fully fueled jet, ready once again to take off and perform its given task. Once that needed physical and emotional rest is achieved, however, like the jet, it's time to move on and take advantage of the time you have.

~Squandering (Wasting) Time on Non-Productive Activities~

Due to the fact that I previously addressed this issue (see chapter 3), I have only to remind you once again that time wasted is time lost, never to be realized again.

If you're not supercharged right now, and you want to get it up and running... you need to look at who you are right now. You have to look at what changes need to be made to take on that supercharged attitude, to fulfill your purposes and your goals.

Ask these questions of yourself, and, after careful thought, *write down your responses*. Use your responses to the questions as a starting point for personal action. Change is not going to take place automatically; you have to initiate it.

Are there certain things that I find myself doing that I need to stop doing?
(Too much television, excessive use of hand-held devices, staying up late, etc.)

_____

_____

*Are there things that I find myself not doing, that
I have to start doing?*
*(Physical exercise, reading, helping other people,
playing games that stimulate learning, etc.)*

_____

_____

*Are there things that I must start doing differently?
(Seek more meaning and purpose in my relationships, improve study habits, spend less needlessly,
etc.)*

_____

_____

Think about it...

- You have the capability to achieve more than you
can imagine, using your own gifts and abilities.

- As you succeed in reaching your goals, your life
may undergo considerable change, forcing you to
extend yourself physically or emotionally beyond
your comfort zone.

- Through the careful planning and visualizing of
goals, the setting of those goals will be more exciting with less anxiety.

- Do not allow past failures and discouragements to hinder your efforts at achieving your goals and dreams.

- Your attitude towards life on a daily basis will influence the decisions you make and will determine how you handle the fear of failure.

- If you want to experience success in achieving your goals, if you long to gain a victory over some area of your life, you need to have an "I Will Not Fail" attitude.

- To fear failure is the same as choosing to fail, because in fearing failure an attempt to succeed may never be made.

5

Set a Target/Goal... Implement a Plan.

IN THE PREVIOUS chapter, I briefly mentioned the need to set goals and encouraged you to lay out a plan to reach those goals. I would now like to spend a bit more time developing this thought, in an effort to more clearly define the means by which goals can be set and realized.

~So Let's Define a Goal~

For starters, we need to consider what a goal actually is. If you were to reference a number of dictionary definitions of the word, there is one overriding theme that repeatedly becomes evident, and that theme is one of an **end**. When you really think about it, in actuality a goal is indeed an end.

Thus a goal can be defined as:

An end result; the conclusion of a purposefully directed effort.

I personally feel more than comfortable with this definition in the context of our discussion; therefore, I will from here on define the word *goal* as just that... an *end*.

Let's think about this for a moment. An end (the goal) cannot take place without a beginning, and you cannot have a beginning and an end without a middle. Now, I recognize that this sounds a bit simplistic, but logic is logic. **Knowing that there is a beginning, a middle, and an end (the goal) can make things much easier as you seek to lay out a plan for achieving objectives in life.**

What Does the Beginning of a Goal Look Like?

There are some things that you need to ponder prior to laying out your personal goals:

- What is your intended purpose for setting the goal?

- Why did a particular goal come to mind anyway?

- How is the goal going to affect you and those with whom you come in contact?

These are actually quite important questions to consider, because in some cases goals can be nothing more than the result of a selfish desire or motive that will be of little or no benefit to you or to anyone else. For example, if you set a goal to date a particular individual simply because he or she is very attractive, and you feel it would make *you* look good being with that person, you need to consider the negatives. The possibility that one or both of you could be hurt emotionally as the result of such a self-centered relationship certainly makes that goal less than worthy. A relationship between a guy and a girl that is founded upon nothing more than external appearances is a relationship that will likely remain shallow and insecure. On the other hand, a relationship that is focused on the heart and personality will be one that is stable and solid. Likewise, if you set a goal to become a millionaire for the sole purpose of buying everything your heart desires, this is nothing more than a self-seeking effort that will ultimately lead to a sense of personal frustration and lack of fulfillment.

Eventually you will face the reality that, unless you are being a help and blessing to others, no amount of "stuff" will bring joy to your life. Someone has wisely said, "If you want to feel rich, just count the things you have that money can't buy."

It will benefit you tremendously to have a clear-cut purpose for setting any particular goal. If you have a goal of some day being a veterinarian, your likely purpose may be to care for and work with animals out of a genuine burden to relieve undue suffering. That is certainly a most worthy purpose. A goal with a noble and defined purpose is a goal that you will, in your heart, feel more driven to accomplish. Think about your purpose; define and clarify your purpose.

Many times when I'm engaging in one-on-one conversations with young people, I find myself asking them the same questions over and over. "What interests do you have?" "What would you love seeing yourself doing in life?" Often these interests are the very building blocks that shape goals; and these goals, when achieved, are potentially the foundation of a life-long career. I truly believe that careers which are the result of previously set goals are the most fulfilling careers of all. When those careers originated through goals that were set because of a fascination or a love for something, how much more fulfilling they must be! Think about it, young person, the possibility of spending the rest of your life engaging in an activity for which you have a deep love and passion. What a joy. What a blessing. There are far too many adults who are desperately frustrated with their jobs. They feel stuck in the midst of day-to-day job responsibilities in which they have absolutely no interest, resulting many times in an actual hatred toward their work. This develops into a life wrought with distress, anger, and resentment. To be engaged each day in an activity that you not only love, but also for which you get paid, is truly priceless. So again I encourage you to take the time to carefully reflect upon your interests, gifts, and passions. Strive to identify specific gifts and abilities that God has given you, for these gifts and abilities were given to you for a purpose. I believe that purpose is **three-fold**.

First, these gifts and skills can be for your own benefit and enjoyment.

To begin with, it matters little what your interests or passions are, for with creativity, imagination, and determination nearly any interest or fascination can be developed and crafted into a successful lifelong career. Please take note that I used the words *creativity, imagination,* and *determination,* for to pursue your dreams is certainly not easy; it's not going to happen unless you make it happen, and that translates into a tremendous amount of hard work and determination. I will discuss this in greater detail in the next chapter. For now, however, guys, you may be thinking... *"Yea, but I love baseball and I'd love to be a professional baseball player. However, I know that the odds are against me that I will ever play professionally, due to the demands being so high. Everyone around me tells me to forget it... it will never happen."* These are the very same thoughts echoing in the minds of countless young people. Indeed, these are very legitimate thoughts, for in reality many individuals have passions that seem so far-fetched and unlikely to occur that the mere thought of them induces an outlook that oozes a sense of hopelessness. I will further address the potential for success as well as failure in chapter 6; but for now, however, you need to reflect upon your motives and how the achievement of these goals will influence you and those around you.

To realize a life-long career, engaging day by day in something that truly gets you excited and something in which you find great delight, as well as something at which you are truly gifted, is a huge joy and benefit to yourself. True happiness and contentment in your work is indeed a great blessing. I like what the writer of Ecclesiastes has to say in chapter 5...

"Moreover, when God gives any man wealth and possessions, and enables him to enjoy them, to accept his lot and be happy in his work-this is a gift of God. He seldom reflects on the days of his life, because God keeps him occupied with gladness of heart."

Ecclesiastes 5:19, 20

To find great enjoyment in your labor and to be involved in something that brings you happiness and fulfillment goes without saying that you as an individual will be better off emotionally, as well as physically. To talk with a person who is really pumped at the thought of going to work on a Monday morning is a very exhilarating and encouraging experience. Unfortunately, these people seem to be few and far between. Too many individuals settle for far less than what their interests and abilities could produce if given the chance. If you as a young person are determined not only to identify your passions, gifts, and abilities, but also to pursue and fulfill them, you will be well on your way to experiencing many a joyful day engaging in work about which you truly get excited... Monday thru Friday! That is indeed a result of being *supercharged!*

Second, these gifts and skills can be for the help and benefit of others.

So what about those around you? How will the achievement of your goals be a help or benefit to other people? Remember that a worthy or beneficial goal needs to be a help to others as well as yourself; it needs to benefit those around you in order for real peace and blessing to be yours.

In considering your goals and achievements, simply ask yourself how others may be encouraged, provided for, or even challenged to achieve their own goals. Your happiness is not an end in itself, for there are millions of others who are struggling in one way or another. You may not be able to benefit millions through the realization of your goals, but, even in touching the lives of a few, your goal would indeed be most worthy, for every life is precious. Keep in mind what I just said, for this conversation will ultimately be concluded (in the last chapter) with examples of young people just like you who are in the process of achieving goals that have been, and will continue to be, a blessing and encouragement to many.

I truly believe that any goal we reach can be of benefit to others if we constantly keep others in mind as we progress toward meeting that goal. If it is our desire to be a doctor, it would seem quite obvious that we will be helping others in doing so. However, what about a professional musician, artist, computer programmer, or auto mechanic? These are also no less worthy achievements, for both doctors and auto mechanics can be a help and encouragement to others; not only by the services they provide, but also through the attitudes displayed while performing those services. As you interact with people whom God brings into your life, you will be given the opportunity to become a part of their lives, and, in being part of their lives, you will be able to influence their attitudes and emotions in a very powerful and effective way. Your attitude will drastically shape their attitude and outlook on life.

Now you may be thinking, "Who is this guy kidding? I'm a teen-ager who's struggling even to pull off a 'C' in math... and he expects me to powerfully affect the lives of others?" If indeed you are currently harboring such thoughts, please accept this simple challenge. Go to a local pond or lake in which the water is very, very calm and glass-like. Pick up a small pebble (the smaller the better) and toss it into the pond. What do you see taking place? That very small pebble is creating ripples that progressively move further and further across the pond. As the ripples move across the pond, they have the tendency to cause other objects to move as well. Look carefully and consider, as leaves, small insects, grass, or anything else that was in contact with the water are now being prompted to move also – if even just slightly. Your seemingly insignificant life can be just like that small pebble! Don't forget, however, that the pebble had to be *put in motion* to have any affect. Decisions that you make, goals you achieve, and dreams you fulfill can and will be an influence on others. So, when you doubt yourself... *simply consider the pebble*.

Use your goals, then, to bring joy and fulfillment into the lives of others, for, who knows, you may end up supercharging *them* as well.

Third, these gifts and skills must be for the honor and glory of God.

"Each one should use whatever gift he has received to serve others, faithfully administering God's grace in its various forms. If anyone speaks, he should do it as one speaking the very words of God. If anyone serves, he should do it with the strength God provides, so that in all things God may be praised through Jesus Christ. To him be the glory and the power for ever and ever. Amen." 1 Peter 4:10-12

My thoughts on this are short and to the point. If, as a teen, you have personally accepted Christ's sacrifice on the cross, you now have the privilege and responsibility of honoring Him through every aspect of your life. It should, therefore, go without saying that, in being a Christian, the fulfillment of your dreams and goals should be with the intent of bringing praise and glory to the King. What an awesome and challenging thought, honoring your Creator with the very skills and abilities that He has instilled within you! Don't take this point lightly, for God's people who willfully squander their gifts and abilities through a self- or people-pleasing attitude, while ignoring or even dishonoring their God, will end up with a less than fulfilling end to their achievements. Because your Creator is worthy of all honor and praise, make it your goal to place Him before all else.

What Does the Middle of a Goal Look Like?

A Plan of Action

Once a goal is set, one needs to consider how he or she will achieve that goal. It is of huge importance that a plan of action be set at this time, or the goal will never be met. How many times have you or someone you know set a New Year's resolution only to give up on it after a few weeks, or even days? I am convinced that the number one reason for not fulfilling a resolution is a failure to lay out a plan of action. No plan of action equals no action at all! Yes, goals can appear to be overwhelming obstacles to conquer. Large goals usually take more time and effort to accomplish than smaller goals. So let's look at it this way; you need to think about a few things concerning the meeting of your goals.

1 - You can set a series of smaller goals that will progressively move you closer to the fulfillment of your ultimate (larger) goal.

2 - You can literally break down the larger goal into "bite size" pieces that will be more easily accomplished. (After all, nobody eats a large pizza all at once... it is typically consumed in smaller, more manageable portions, one slice at a time. *Alright, give me the benefit of the doubt here, for I'm sure that someone* *somewhere on this planet is able to consume a large pizza without ever stopping for a breath. However, I would have to classify that individual as **non**-human.)*

3 - You must write your goals down.

4 - Seek an individual (or individuals) who can challenge, support and encourage you in the fulfillment of your goals.

~Setting Smaller Goals~

   Let's first consider the idea of **setting a series of smaller goals in order to reach the large goal**. Allow me to give you a simple example of this. Suppose you are a guy who enjoys lifting weights and has set a personal goal to bench press 350 pounds within one year. You are currently maxing out at 275 pounds. A 75 pound increase in a twelve month period initially seems almost too much to imagine. However, through the setting of smaller, specific goals, the increased physical strength can be developed, which will then enable you to reach the 350 pound mark. Here are a few examples of specific goals that can be set in order to reach this particular goal.

- I will increase the weight of my standing barbell shoulder presses by 3 pounds each month over a period of 12 months (to develop shoulder strength).

- I will increase the weight of my barbell leg squats by 5 pounds each month throughout the 12 month period (to develop leg and core body strength).

- I will do an extra set of dumbbell curls over the 12 month period (to develop bicep strength).

- I will do an extra set of triceps push-downs over the 12 month period (to develop strength in the triceps).

- I will add heavy dumbbell bench presses to my regular workout routine each week (to add another dimension of resistance to my bench press regimen).

Please understand what these 5 specific goals are meant to accomplish. Each of the 5 goals, as they are realized, will ultimately lend to the strengthening and developing of the muscles required to successfully build you up to reaching the 350 pound bench press goal. Because these goals are less intense and demanding on your body (and your mind), you will more likely be able to pull them off and thus reach your ultimate goal. This strategy can be applied to any particular goal which you may set, whether it be an educational, physical, financial, or career goal.

The thing to keep in mind is that even a giant can be brought down, simply by breaking one leg at a time.

~Breaking the Larger Goal into "Bite Size" Pieces~

We'll go back and re-use the example of the 350 pound bench press goal. Remember that an increase of 75 pounds needs to take place in order to reach this goal. This is a considerable amount of weight, therefore, it may have the tendency to overwhelm you and cause you to give up before you begin. Because failure isn't an option, we need to conquer this giant in the least stressful way possible... by breaking his legs one at a time. This isn't rocket science, so let's just do some simple math.

If we take the 75 pound increase goal and divide it by 52 weeks, we get an unimpressive (and much less intimidating) 1.44 pounds per week.

Now sit back for a moment and digest this. Would you prefer to tackle a 75 pound goal or a 1.44 pound goal? No brainer here! And the cool thing about this is that, like the previous example, it can be applied to conquer any major goal... from preparing for a final exam to saving up for a sports car.

I do need to take a breather here and make something very clear. The examples I've presented are for the sole purpose of clarifying and simplifying the means by which major, seemingly unattainable goals can be accomplished. I've done this so that anyone, anywhere, can understand the fact that you *can* set large goals... and you *can* reach those goals! Far too many people (including myself) have purposefully declined from setting large goals because they failed to think about and develop a plan to lead them to successfully reaching those goals. Without a simplified plan of attack, we tend to view the monster as something that is too large to conquer.

"When you change the way you look at things, the things you look at change".

Wayne Dyer

~Write Down Your Goals~

You will benefit greatly by taking the time to carefully consider and write down your goals. Grab a piece of paper large enough to list your goals very specifically. It may help to use a piece of paper that, because of its color or size, will have the tendency to attract your attention to it every time you go near it! Yes, that sounds a bit strange, but the whole idea is constantly to remind yourself of your goals. If your goals are not "in your face," you may overlook or forget them. If you overlook or forget them, you will lose your drive and focus... and that's not a good thing!

Advertisers purposefully bombard the consumer with commercials that are both impressionable and repetitive, resulting in the imprinting of that product into our minds. It's a strategy that works for them, and it will for you as well... so *write down your goals*.

Yes, goals need to be put on paper, but how they are written can be very powerful as well. As you can see from the examples that I've given above, I purposefully used *two* words consistently. Those words are "I" and "will." To personalize your goals with an "I" will serve to remind you that it is *you and you only* who can bring them to pass. Nobody will work on *your* goals for you. The other word is "will." In emphasizing that you *will* accomplish this or that, in essence you are commanding yourself to work toward that end. It is *you* holding *yourself* accountable. You are not giving yourself a choice as to whether or not you plan on reaching that goal. In your mind it's already a done deal!

~*Find Someone to Stand with You*~

Next, it may be a help to you to seek an individual (or individuals) who will challenge, support, and encourage you in the fulfillment of your goals.

Be careful, however, whom you choose. These *must* be people who are supercharged as well, individuals who will constantly be ready and willing to offer encouraging and supportive words and advice. Choosing someone who is not motivated will be of no help to you, because it requires motivation in order to motivate. It has been wisely suggested that you cannot expect to soar like an eagle if you're grounded with turkeys.

It will also be to your benefit if you surround yourself with those who have successfully accomplished the exact thing for which you are striving. If it's your goal to be a professional artist, by all means get involved and surround yourself with professional artists. Ask questions. Allow their expertise to positively influence your development and creativity as an artist.

Before we move on to the next chapter, let's consider some major points we've just covered.

Think about it...

- A goal is the conclusion of a purposefully directed effort.

- Each person has his or her own reason for setting any particular goal.

- The benefit of achieving a goal is threefold...
    1) your own benefit and enjoyment,
    2) the benefit and help of others,
    3) the honor and glory of God.

- Large goals can be broken down into smaller, more manageable ones.

- The writing down of your goals (get specific) has tremendous value.

- Surround yourself with those who can help you to achieve your goals.

6

Hard Work, Obstacles, Frustration, and Failure... Prepare to Get Knocked Around!

SETTING A SPECIFIC goal in life can be likened to an eagle soaring high above the ground in an effort to spot a small rodent below. Though the bird is a great distance from its prey, its tremendous eyesight still enables it to focus on that prey, while ignoring all the distractions between him and it. So it is with your goals. Though they may be in the distant future, you need to focus on those goals, overcoming the many distractions and hindrances that can potentially rob you of your vision. As the eagle draws nearer to its prey, its focus grows in intensity until finally the prey is successfully within the firm grasp of its talons. This perfectly exemplifies the focus and intensity with which goals can be achieved in your life. This same focus and intensity is what drives a supercharged individual; this same focus and intensity is what will likewise drive you as a super-charged teen.

I wrote the above statement one day while dwelling upon the magnificence of an eagle in flight. As I thought more and more about the intensity with which an eagle hunts its prey, the greater I realized just how focused and intense we must be in seeking to achieve our goals.

You have likely figured it out by now that the fulfillment of your dreams and goals is not going to be an easy task. How hard you work at achieving those goals depends entirely upon how important that goal is to you. That is the reason why I previously mentioned your need to carefully consider your goals. A goal that is set in an effort to fulfill a deep seated personal fascination or passion is a goal that will drive you on until that goal is met. On the other hand, a goal that is set in order to satisfy a passing, short term interest will likely never be met, due to a lack of determination and willpower.

With this said, let's now move on. Assuming that your goals have been set and you have laid out a specific plan for achieving them, it's now time to face some realities. The realities are that you will need to be ready to...

- Work Very Hard,

- Encounter Many Obstacles,

- Face Frustration and Failure.

Let's now carefully consider each one of these realities in some detail, for there is no question that you will indeed be running headlong into them at some time or another during your quest for the achievement of your goals. Even though these realities appear to be downright scary on the surface, the fact is that each one of them can without doubt be overcome.

~Work Very Hard~

The realization of a goal requires focus. The realization of a goal demands intensity. Hard work is at the core of any successful endeavor, from learning how to ride a bike, to successfully completing high-school, to establishing and maintaining personal relationships. Hard work is truly a reality that every human being needs to face. Before we even consider the subject of hard work, however, there immediately comes to mind *two* key factors that will determine to what degree you or anyone else will actually be able to work. Get ready to cringe, because as far as I'm aware, not many teenagers get overly excited about either one. But I see the need to throw them at you anyway. So... here we go...

- *Exercise,*

- *Proper Rest.*

Ouch! I know that probably hurts quite a few of you reading this, but the reality of it is that the human body operates at its peak potential when these two conditions are met. *(Actually there are three... the other is proper nutrition and diet... but, since you are a young person, I will spare you of that one.)* Now, I will purposefully not dwell on this subject at any length, however I do see the need to address it for your own benefit. I am fully aware of the fact that many young people thrive on being physically fit for any number of reasons. Many are involved in high school sports that demand a high level of physical fitness, while others simply enjoy the benefits of looking "good" as a result of exercise. However, I also am aware that a large percentage of youth (as well as adults) give little or no consideration to the need for or benefit of regular exercise. The truth is that exercise combined with proper rest *(and nutrition)* is exactly what is required for maximum performance, that is, physical, emotional, and intellectual performance. You were probably not expecting me to throw this in your face, and, truthfully, I was not even anticipating mentioning it; however, we've gone this far, so I may as well address the issue. Allow me to go on.

There is a good bit of research that emphasizes the benefits of proper exercise and rest when it comes to physical, emotional, and intellectual performance; and the results of this research should not be ignored. If you are really serious about supercharging yourself, you need to be ready and willing to attend to the needs of the very body that will be supercharged.

As far as exercise is concerned, the mind and body benefit immensely in a number of areas. As you engage in any aerobic exercise, more blood is pumped throughout your body, including to your brain. Brain tissue is then nourished by this oxygen-rich blood, resulting in a more efficiently functioning brain. A brain that functions well is a brain with enhanced memory, attention, and learning capabilities. Furthermore, the benefits of exercise to the mind include reduced stress, as well as a lack of mood and behavioral swings... which obviously results in enhanced social skills. If the goals you are seeking to accomplish are physically demanding, exercise may not only reduce the risk of injury, but also aid in the efficiency of your physical performance.

Now that we've considered exercise, what about the benefits of sufficient sleep?

Once again, research suggests that sleep not only helps an individual's immune system but also benefits the cardiovascular functions which may relate to heart disease and strokes. Furthermore, sufficient sleep can reduce stress as well as improve memory. I could go on, but I believe you got the point. I would challenge you to do additional research in these areas, especially if you find yourself slacking off or struggling with either of these important considerations.

In getting get back to the subject of hard work, however, I feel we need to clarify what "hard work" actually is. I believe that hard work is *any activity which we perform, in which we are directly challenged in any way*. Studying can be hard work, along with digging a hole, running a marathon, babysitting children, or learning to drive a car. If you are seeking to accomplish a particular task, and you find yourself being challenged, stretched, or even struggling, it's safe to say that you are facing something that can be defined as hard work.

"Opportunity is missed by most people because it is dressed in overalls and looks like work."

Thomas A. Edison

Hard work is the very reason why so many people purposefully avoid making drastic decisions in life, even though those decisions may ultimately result in their realizing true fulfillment and happiness. It's so much easier to do things that are easy. Unfortunately, taking the easy way out typically results in an individual just "blending in" with the hordes of others who decided to do the same thing. There is no question about it; those individuals who defeat the "easy way out" mentality are usually the ones who are admired or looked up to in one way or another. From high school and college graduates to the rich and famous and everyone in between, we tend to respect those who have accomplished something that we have not.

So, once again it appears as though we have come face-to-face with a "giant" that needs to be conquered. Previously, when we faced such a giant, we simply brought him down by breaking one leg at a time – so why not do it again? We need to overcome hard work by simply viewing it as a series of different areas that we need to address and engage.

These areas are...

- *Courage,*

- *Self-Discipline,*

- *Education,*

- *Relationships.*

These few areas are by no means all there are as we tackle the subject of hard work, but they are more than sufficient for our discussion at this time. As we briefly consider each of the above, keep in mind that all of these areas, in and of themselves, include hard work. It's something that can not be ignored, but can indeed be overcome and accepted.

Courage

I have come across a number of sources that strive to define courage. Actually, courage is a lot of things; therefore, there are many ways to describe it, all of which are likely correct. Because I like to keep things relatively simple, I will define courage as nothing more than forcing yourself to do what you *know* you *should* do. It's going beyond that which is comfortable for you, going into areas in which the outcome is unknown. Courage seems to come in waves, and sometimes the waves are large and spectacular; other times it just meets the need of the moment. There's the courage that wells up within an individual, enabling him to enter a burning building to save a child; on the other hand, there's also the courage that enables a person to ask, "Will you marry me?"

Each and every human being has God-given courage within. We often cannot control those situations or circumstances that require courage, but we can indeed control how we respond when those circumstances arise. Throughout your life your courage within will rise to the occasion as is required, but I truly believe it needs to be purposefully exercised as often as necessary so that it actually becomes habitual in nature. Yes, I personally believe a person can develop courage, just as a weight lifter develops muscle. If you courageously pursue your passions and goals, fully believing that success is possible, not only will goals be met, but, as you continue to establish additional goals, you will experience a ripple effect in which courage is just a natural part of what drives you to further achievements. (At this point, by the way, you would now be experiencing the state of being supercharged!)

I always try to refrain from applying the overused term, "out of your comfort zone." At this point, however, I feel it to be most appropriate to our discussion because the realization of your goals will often demand that you leave your "comfort zone." This "zone" is nothing more than a place of emotional, physical, intellectual, or financial security. It's a place we like to call "home." It's a place wherein we find familiarity and contentment, a place we so often simply do not want to leave. If this is the case, why is it that some people purposefully leave it? Why risk wandering away from so comfortable an existence? These are good questions that have a very real and practical answer... it's called *vision*. Vision in itself is made up of dreams, passions, and interests that lie within the depths of each individual. Vision is the catalyst that forces us to create, pursue, and achieve our goals. However, vision without courage is like a bicycle without pedals, for it is courage that propels you forward.

By this time, you should more clearly understand that courage is a very crucial tool for facing the hard work "giant." Before we move on, however, I would like to challenge you to personally and purposefully work on exercising and developing courage every chance you get. You've got it; the Lord provides it... you just need to take the initiative to tap into His reserve.

Self-Discipline

Many individuals, upon being presented with the subject of self-discipline, would likely prefer simply to hold their hands over their ears and run the other direction as though being pursued by a hungry lion. The thought of self-discipline, the mere mention of the term, to many people has the same effect as the screeching of fingernails across a chalk board or the unexpected slithering snake in the grass. Ok, I'll admit that the word seems to implicate a type of self-torture in which pain, suffering, and even death are the inevitable outcomes. But, come on, let's get realistic here; though there may be a degree of discomfort, pain, or frustration involved with self-discipline, it is absolutely nothing to be feared or avoided. Most of the time it proves to be of huge benefit to the person who employs it.

So what exactly is self-discipline, and how can it be of benefit to you? Self-discipline is nothing more than a person's ability to take action regardless of whether or not that person wants to take action at that time. Simply put, it's doing something that you feel needs to be done, even if you don't feel like doing it at the time. It carries with it a sense of consistency, dedication, and diligence. It can be applied to any situation in life, from brushing your teeth to doing your homework to working toward fulfilling your wildest dreams and goals. Yes, self-discipline needs to be an active part in the life of every person.

"What are the benefits?" you might ask. I believe the benefits are many. Here are a few:

- *Creating a good work ethic,*

- *Creating good study habits,*

- *Developing good relationships,*

- *Overcoming addictions,*

- *Overcoming procrastination,*

- *Reaching any goal.*

These are but a few examples; however, the point I want to emphasize is the fact that self-discipline is a very powerful tool in the hands of those who have it. Once again, self-discipline is much like courage in that it must be practiced; it must be exercised. You must train yourself to consistently apply self-discipline to every aspect of your life. The overwhelming, all-powerful emotion that seemingly sneaks into the life of every individual is a lack of motivation. De-motivation is an enemy that holds so many dreams, goals, and aspirations in a captive, prisoner-like state. Self-discipline, on the other hand, is the super hero that can defeat that enemy and deliver those captives, setting them free so that they can be fully expressed and realized.

It's very easy to tell yourself and everyone else that you are going to be exercising every day after school. Words are cheap! However it takes a huge amount of discipline to actually make it happen, especially if you are tired and hungry. The temptation to kick up your feet and relax after a long day at school can be overwhelming. You know within your heart that you would benefit from your planned exercise routine, and you feel angry with yourself for not going through with it. Self-discipline can be bolstered by constantly reminding yourself of the benefits of sticking to your plan. Write down those benefits. Keep them at a place where you will be constantly reminded of them. Imagine the excitement and pride you will experience as you see your diligence paying off. Visualize the incredible feeling of self-satisfaction that you will gain as the result of daily fulfilling your exercise goals. Convince yourself to stick with it, and eventually the visualization will become a reality.

I used exercise as a simple example here, but these same principles can be applied to any plans or goals you may make for yourself, whether they involve diet, relationships, studying, or change of habits.

Consider self-discipline; grasp it, develop it, enjoy it, and benefit from it. It's yours for the taking!

Education

You may be wondering what education may have to do with hard work. Keep in mind that we are looking at specific areas that will help you to overcome and successfully get through the hard work that you will be facing as you strive to reach your goals. Education, or *the purposeful pursuit of knowledge, understanding, and experience*, will undoubtedly be of great benefit to you as you face the reality of hard work. If your goal is to become a physical education teacher, it is a no-brainer that your studies would include that of physical exercise and nutrition. If you are striving to be a clothing designer, you would necessarily have to gain a deeper understanding of various styles and sewing techniques as well as the vast array of differing fabrics.

These are quite obvious examples; however, what I am trying to emphasize is the benefit of going above and beyond the traditional education in which so many engage. Taking the effort to read, read, and read some more will reap huge rewards in one's gaining knowledge as he or she pursues interests or goals. The good news is that it is always easier to go all out in your studies if you are focusing your studies on those topics that are related to your passions and interests.

A simple and straightforward example of the point I'm trying to make is something like this. You may want to be something as odd and crazy as a roller coaster designer. You absolutely love the thrill of the ride, but you also have a fascination with how roller coasters work and how they are designed. You may know all the statistics of the various coasters from parks around the world, from the different speeds, heights, lengths, or number of inversions even to the maximum vertical angle of the individual drops. As impressive and awe-inspiring as these facts may be, even if one masters an understanding of every conceivable statistic, there's a whole lot more to being a roller coaster designer. One needs to be thoroughly trained in structural or mechanical engineering, physics, mathematics, and design software. These are obviously subjects that will involve college training; however, one can secure a significant head-start in these studies simply by taking the time and making the effort to begin research while in high school. Explain your goals to your teachers or guidance counselors, who would be able to suggest books, magazines, or seminars that would serve to educate you in these areas. If this sounds like a lot of hard work, that's because it *is* a lot of hard work. In most cases, you have to put tremendous effort into getting what you want. There is no shortage of people who have the dream of becoming roller coaster designers. There is, however, a shortage of available positions in this area of employment. That translates into the need for you to be as fully educated and prepared as you can possibly be, so that you will stand out among the many individuals competing for that same position. It's certainly not impossible, but you definitely need to do your homework to make it a reality in your own life.

Again I want to stress that though a college education may be in your future, the need to take the initiative to learn begins now. The greater the emphasis you place on educating yourself now, the better off you will be when attending college or any other learning program related to your future plans and goals. There is no shortage of books or other media for you of which to take advantage In your effort to learn and grow. Obviously, the internet is a vast source of knowledge. However, the local library is likewise loaded with media ready to be indulged.

"An investment in knowledge pays the best interest." Benjamin Franklin

Don't sell yourself short in reaching your goals due to a lack of knowledge or understanding. Don't think that you are too young to do research for your own personal growth and development. The knowledge you gain now will benefit you throughout your entire life. In addition, the more you know the more valuable you will be to other people. The more that people can rely upon your skills and understanding, the greater benefit you will be to them. This translates into more and better job opportunities. Passion combined with knowledge and understanding will go a long way in enabling you to enjoy the benefits of reaching your goals. Always strive to develop yourself intellectually.

Make the effort to purposefully set time aside for reading, research, and learning – for as you do so, you will be building the muscles of intellect, which will enable you to power your way up and over the mountain of hard work that you will inevitably face as you seek to achieve your goals.

Relationships

The story is told of a farmer who planted a field of pumpkins. As the pumpkins were growing, the farmer would regularly walk up and down the rows of the field, checking their progress. One day he stumbled upon a glass jug lying among the young pumpkins, and he figured he would do an experiment. He forced a small, young pumpkin through the opening of the jug and into the jug itself. Then he set down the jug with the pumpkin and walked away. Weeks later, while once again checking the pumpkins in the field, he came across the jug. He was surprised to find that the young pumpkin within the jug had completely grown to fill the jug, and that it had actually conformed to the shape of the jug into which it had previously been placed. Upon breaking the glass jug to further inspect the pumpkin, he realized that the growth of the pumpkin had been prevented above and beyond what the confines of the jug would allow. The glass jug not only prevented the pumpkin from reaching its full potential, but it also forced it into a shape that was quite unnatural for that pumpkin.

And so it is with people. Because of the environment in which we live, or the relationships in which we are involved, our personal growth is often stunted or discouraged. And, like the pumpkin, our very outlook on life and our personalities can be shaped by that same environment or those same relationships. This so frequently results not only in our never reaching our full God-given potential, but also in our never even trying.

"A man only learns in two ways, one by reading, and the other by association with smarter people."
Will Rogers

The world in which you and I live contains no shortage of opportunity. Opportunity to express ourselves, our gifts, our passions, and our abilities is limited only by the degree to which we allow ourselves to be held back. We frequently so want to be accepted by others that we actually allow them literally to control our lives. Our thoughts and desires are often held under lock and key in an effort to find acceptance within our group. If you find yourself regularly engaging with friends who would question your desire to better yourself or to develop yourself... maybe its time to seek out relationships in which you not only would feel free to express yourself, but also would be encouraged and challenged to do so. You need to purposefully surround yourself with friends that display a supercharged mentality about life, friends who are driven to better themselves physically, intellectually, financially, and certainly spiritually. These individuals are the ones who will more likely influence you in a positive way by stretching you to the point of personal growth, development, and fulfillment. Herein lies exactly what is required to break through the barrier of hard work successfully, which will then open wide the path to the realization of your goals and dreams.

~Encounter Many Obstacles~
"One way or the other, if you want to find reasons why you shouldn't keep on, you'll find 'em. The obstacles are all there; there are a million of 'em." Benny Goodman

The truth contained within these words of Benny Goodman ring oh so true. Obstacles seem to be capable of reproducing themselves at a rate even beyond that of rabbits. The encouraging thing about obstacles is that they can be overcome. Unfortunately, we all too often fail to remember this, and the result is that we lose confidence and give up. The way we view obstacles will determine how we will deal with them when they arise. If we allow them to stop us in our tracks and prevent us from moving on, it is likely that we will have a very negative and even fearful view of them. If, on the other hand, we diligently work around them, even if it involves a change in plans, it is likely that we will view them as nothing more than a stepping stone to success. Indeed that is what they need to be viewed as – stepping stones that must be encountered in order to get us to where we are going.

"I have not failed. I've just found 10,000 ways that won't work." Thomas Edison

Far too many people, myself included, have allowed obstacles or setbacks to completely derail their plans. That is nothing more than time wasted. As a child progresses from crawling to standing up and, finally, to taking that first step, obstacles are inevitable. I have never met a parent who purposefully stopped a child from learning how to walk because he or she kept falling. All parents recognize that falling is a natural occurrence as a child develops the coordination and strength needed for walking. Even though the child struggles and seemingly fails time and time again, eventually the first steps are taken and then there's no looking back.

What do obstacles look like anyway?

Obstacles come in a countless variety of forms, most of which are so obvious to you that you can hardly miss them. They all, however, have one common attribute. They all have the tendency to cause you to feel frustrated, rejected, or discouraged. Obstacles make your heart sink. You feel defeated, as though you did all that you could, but it still wasn't enough. Some obstacles do indeed slow up your progress, robbing you of your drive and determination. On a positive note, however, the loss of drive and determination need not be permanent. The motivation to move on with a renewed zeal and drive can be experienced once again as you refocus on your goal as well as seek encouragement from others. Though some obstacles may take the form of monsters, many times one need only to turn on the lights of creativity and imagination and the monster will disappear.

How do you deal with obstacles?

Any way that you look at it, obstacles exist whether we like it or not. Think about it for a moment... how boring and unchallenging would life be if there were no such thing as obstacles? There would be countless millionaires and loads of professional athletes. Every man and woman alive would be in tip-top physical shape. Success would be so commonplace that it wouldn't even be called success any longer, because everyone would have it. We would all be fully content and at peace with ourselves... or would we? I think not! Human beings need to be challenged, or their God-given gifts and abilities would never be exercised. There would be no need for a super-charged drive within, if everything were simply handed to us without any effort or challenges. We need to be honest with ourselves, and with life in general. Obstacles exist – so how do we deal with them?

I believe you can deal with obstacles in three ways.

1 – Admit to yourself that obstacles do indeed exist.

In the area of the country where I live, on a hot, humid summer day, the threat of thunderstorms is always present. Needless to say, when we engage in any outdoor activities (picnic, bike riding, hiking, etc.), we are always aware of this threat. We do not... indeed, we *cannot*... pretend that storms will never hit us. We have experienced them many times before, therefore we know without a doubt that they not only exist, but, if the conditions are right, we will most likely experience one. This is the same attitude you must have concerning obstacles in reaching your goals. Simply put... prepare yourself, because they're going to happen!

2 - Determine what the potential obstacles will be.

Since you know your goals, you should be able to identify what obstacles to expect. If we use the thunderstorm example again, it can be easily understood that, if you are planning an outdoor picnic on a hot and humid summer day, thunderstorms would be an obvious potential obstacle. Likewise, you may want to consider the likelihood of sunburn, mosquitoes, and flies. At a picnic any or all of these threats are certainly possible. An athlete, on the other hand, would benefit from being aware of the possibility of injury, dehydration, or any other threat that may hinder his or her ability to perform to the fullest potential. And so it is with any activity in which one engages; obstacles are everywhere.

3 - Pre-plan on how to deal with these obstacles and overcome them.

Now that you have a pretty good idea of what the likely obstacles may look like, it's time to take action against them. Even at this stage of the game, before the obstacles appear, you can prepare to defeat them. So, in following the example of the picnic, one needs only to prepare for the expected threats by laying out a plan and getting some things together. With the possibility of thunderstorms, you may prepare to gather together quickly in a garage. The garage must be free from anything that would prevent everyone from entering; therefore, if at all possible, it would likely be cleaned out in advance. Likewise, with the threat of sunburn, mosquitoes, and flies, one should prepare to have sunscreen, citronella candles, and a fly-swatter or two available. Once again, allow me to apply the example of the athlete. If injury or dehydration is a possibility, one needs perhaps to prepare in advance by thoroughly stretching and engaging in warm-up exercises, as well as ensuring that proper hydration is always a priority.

I do realize that these examples are over-simplified. These examples, however, are meant to get my point across as clearly as possible; *obstacles are real... so anticipate and prepare for them!*

~Face Frustration and Failure~

Last, but not least, I feel we need to address the reality of bumps and bruises. The bumps and bruises to which I'm referring aren't necessarily of the physical kind. In the pursuit of goals and achievements, we run the risk of facing emotional struggles, challenges, and failures. These hardships are often the result of obstacles... obstacles that simply wear us down not only physically, but emotionally as well. You may have worked very hard to try out for a sports team in school, only to be rejected because you weren't quite good enough to make the team. You may be ridiculed by friends because of a choice you made that was not viewed as popular among them. Or perhaps you received a poor grade on an exam for which you spent countless hours preparing. All of these scenarios hurt and they hurt a lot. Even though you can prepare for most obstacles and eventually overcome them, sometimes they leave scars. Life, indeed, has its share of frustrations, and, in the pursuit of one's goals, these frustrations may leave you feeling hopelessly defeated.

All successful people have had to deal with more failures and frustrations than they would care to admit. I use the term failures, not to imply defeat, but simply to emphasize the fact that so often, if something can go wrong, it will. Many wealthy entrepreneurs experienced numerous failures until they finally realized true success. Their success was founded upon nothing less than the experience they gained as a result of previous failures. Failures teach us, define us, and shape us into the individuals we need to be in order to achieve greater things. Indeed, failure is not a word that anyone likes to hear, especially when it is being applied to him. No matter how much we envision failure as being the end of the road for us, it always can and will serve to further strengthen and enable us. When a plan does not come together, when you get stopped in your tracks, it will only turn into a failure if *you* allow it to do so. In understanding failure as a step toward success, your chances of achieving that success will increase dramatically.

*"**Success is a journey, not a destination. The doing is often more important than the outcome.**" Arthur Ashe*

You can experience success every day by viewing setbacks and failures as individual steps on that journey. If the path of success in accomplishing a particular goal can be likened to a walk on the beach, with one end of the beach representing a starting point and the far end of the beach being the actual goal (successfully being met), take note of what is in between. In between there are many footprints in the sand that represent each day that you actually took a step forward in progression toward that goal. ***Steps must be taken one after another to get to the other end of the beach… likewise, steps must be taken <u>daily</u> to progress toward your goal… or you will never realize success in reaching that goal.***

In the last chapter I will be sharing with you some true stories of supercharged young people just like you, individuals who are doing all the hard work and facing all the frustrations that go along with achieving one's goals. These examples are real and serve to make it very clear that they, like you, are fully equipped to excel in life. The victory is theirs. The victory can also be yours.

In living your life to the fullest and utilizing the gifts and abilities that your Creator has instilled within you – always pushing harder, daring to dream bigger, challenging yourself with ever-increasing fervor, and never giving up – you will be experiencing the full power of the supercharger within. You, as a young person, have the potential to achieve much more than can ever be imagined, fulfilling your own passions, being a help and blessing to countless people, and, above all else, honoring the God who alone has equipped and enabled you to do it.

So there you have it! Give it all you've got! Super-charge yourself!

Think about it...

- Hard work and a mindset to accomplish it are absolutely necessary for you to achieve your goals.

- Courage is a crucial element in overcoming the apprehension and fear that prevents so many from not only setting goals, but achieving them as well.

- Courage, residing within each of us, is like a muscle that can be exercised and developed so that it becomes a regular part of who we are.

- Self-discipline, doing something that you feel needs to be done even if you don't feel like doing it, needs to be constantly applied in life in order for one's dreams to become reality.

- Educate yourself; for the knowledge you acquire now will benefit you throughout your entire life. If you have an interest or passion for something, that passion combined with knowledge and understanding will be valuable in enabling you to find fulfillment in that area of interest.

- Don't allow obstacles to frustrate or stop you from achieving your goals. You must view them for what they are - stepping stones on the path that will get you to where you are going.

- Failures are what we make of them. Accept them as lessons to teach you, define you, and shape you into the individual you need to be in order to achieve greater things.

7

The Sweetness of Victory

IN THIS LAST chapter of our conversation, it's time to bring everything together. We've covered a number of different topics from considering your value as an individual to setting personal goals and everything in between. Through it all I have tried to impress upon you, as a young person, the importance of dwelling upon and applying these basic truths in order to experience personal fulfillment and to be a blessing and help to others, all the while honoring the Creator God.

At this point you may be wondering if all this stuff works. Does the identifying of my gifts and abilities and the setting of goals work? Is the likelihood of failure and rejection in the process of reaching my goals worth the frustration and effort? The answer is an overwhelming *yes*! Many individuals throughout history have worked hard and long to fulfill their dreams and ambitions, proving to themselves and the world that planning and effort produce results. These results are felt and experienced by you and me on a daily basis, even though we may not be aware of it. Nearly all of what we enjoy today is due to the massive efforts of others, individuals like Thomas Edison, Henry Ford, Walt Disney, Sam Walton, and countless others.

As successful as these individuals have been and as much as they have contributed to those around them, the purpose of this conversation is not to focus on the efforts and achievements of such people. (I would strongly encourage you to read the stories of those who have achieved their personal financial, physical, spiritual, or intellectual goals. There are many, and their stories can be a huge encouragement to those seeking the same.) Rather, I want to make it much more personal, much more understandable and real to you as a young person. Therefore, the individuals I will be profiling here are young people who at the time of this writing are in the very process of reaching for their dreams and goals. They are exemplifying the supercharged spirit that is the foundation of this entire conversation. Each of these young people is an incredible example of a teen *just like you* who absolutely refuses to conform to the average standards of those around him. These are real people with real goals, who are overcoming the negative influences that are imposed upon them by a society of individuals cast from the mold of mediocrity.

Read their stories and embrace the fact that you are fully free and equipped to follow their examples, for you, like them, hold the key to the supercharger within you.

Olivia Gusti

It's what many a little girl's dreams are made of; the graceful movements of a ballerina gliding effortlessly across the stage to the admiration and applause of a delighted audience. This is without a doubt one of the most awe-inspiring thoughts that a young girl can envision. In the eyes of many, it defines the very essence of girlhood through the display of grace, elegance, and poise. Many young ladies have the opportunity to get a taste of their dreams through dance lessons, allowing them to experience the joys of expressing themselves through movement, and it is in this that Olivia Gusti is no exception.

Beginning dance lessons at four years of age, Olivia shared in the same excitement and wonder of countless young girls who have enjoyed this experience. It was not too long, however, until her dance instructors came to the realization that there was something unique about Olivia, a giftedness that prompted their attention. It appeared to them and to her parents that Olivia had the natural God-given ability to express herself through the movements of dance. The lessons progressed and became increasingly more challenging, and as a young girl Olivia became frustrated and discouraged. Never one to give up, she continued on, however, though with a downcast and, at times, negative mindset.

Likewise, at this time Olivia was studying and enjoying piano. With conflicting interests of both dance and piano lessons, Olivia was forced to make a choice. She was going to give it her all regardless of her decision.

Always one to push herself, her creativity, and her abilities, she knew that this decision might very well define her future. With the support and encouragement of parents and family, and with an unwavering trust in God, she chose to pursue dance and to pursue it with a passion. She came to the conclusion that this was it; she was giving it everything she had. Her supercharged mindset of diligence and persistence that was always part of who she was in the past, would enable her to achieve even the most lofty of goals in the future. She believed it, and she was going for it. Thus it was, at the age of eleven, that Olivia took on a serious and renewed mindset, a mindset that would prompt a series of exciting events and opportunities, enabling her to advance above and beyond her original expectations.

As time passed, and her dance skills developed to an ever higher level of technical, creative, and artistic complexity, she has refused to waver in her diligence, perseverance, and zeal. Practicing up to six hours a day, sacrificing opportunities with friends and family, all while balancing a heavy home-schooling schedule, she has maintained an attitude of thankfulness and duty to family, friends, and God. Having faced and overcome various frustrations along the way, Olivia has continued moving forward with the supercharged and positive mindset that is so necessary in reaching one's goals. When asked about any concerns or anxieties of what her future may hold, she has made it very clear that she is neither nervous nor afraid, for she realizes that her family, her friends and her Lord will provide the needed support and encouragement. Olivia has maintained a never-give-up attitude, believing fully that through the use of her God-given gifts and abilities, as well as through great effort and consistency, dreams and goals can indeed be met.

At the time of this writing, at only fifteen years of age, Olivia has performed in numerous classical ballet productions including the Nutcracker, Giselle, Coppelia, Snow White and the Seven Dwarfs, Paquita, Swan Lake, and Cinderella. She has, likewise, competed in the Youth America Grand Prix Semi-Finals in Tampa, Florida, where she placed first in contemporary and within the top twelve in classical. She followed that with the Grand Prix Finals in New York City, where, though failing to place, she progressed through three rounds and was offered a full scholarship with academics to the Palucca School of Dresden in Germany, one of the top dance schools in the world. She has also recently completed a five week summer intensive training with the Pacific Northwest Ballet in Washington State.

While her future looks positive, Olivia still takes nothing for granted. She realizes that continued hard work, perseverance, and support from many individuals is the only means by which she will ultimately realize the fulfillment of her dreams and goals. Her future plans? Touring with a dance company in Europe, perhaps in Stuttgart, Germany, which is among the top four in the world. Yes, a lofty... but *attainable*... goal, especially for a *supercharged* teen like Olivia Gusti.

Ryan Neiswender

As far as accomplishments, dreams, and goals are concerned, a person's attitude can make the difference between trying and not trying, between success and failure. To dwell upon one's limitations can have the same negative affect as a suit of armor on a long-distance runner; try as he may, the constant reminder of its presence will be burdensome and debilitating, hindering the speed and agility needed to be competitive. To the shame of many, these limitations are often self-imposed, the result of a negative and self-abasing mindset. For those with true physical limitations and disabilities, the daily tasks of life may be not only frustrating, but difficult as well. In the case of many of these individuals, little physical activity is engaged in beyond that which is absolutely necessary for meeting one's daily needs. Such is not the case with Ryan Neiswender.

At only 19 years of age, Ryan has been more competitive, pushed himself harder, and realized more personal victories than many individuals experience in an entire lifetime. His motivation to excel and to be the very best at everything he does was part of who he was from the very beginning. As a child growing up Ryan enjoyed competitive athletic activities just like his friends, including micro-soccer and t-ball, which require a degree of mobility and skill. He always gave everything he had, both physically and emotionally, in any activity in which he found himself engaged.

In many ways Ryan, with his competitive and driven personality, is absolutely no different than any other teenager. There is, however, one significant difference; Ryan was born with a congenital muscle disorder which affected his legs. As a result, he is lacking his quadriceps, the large extensor muscle of the front of the thigh. Although he is unable to support himself without the use of leg braces, Ryan's intense motivation to excel has always enabled him to hold his own regardless of the physical challenges he has faced, from going to the mall with his friends to playing even the most intensely competitive sports. Right from the start it was decided by his parents that his disability was not going to hold him back, thus neither they, nor his family or friends, ever looked at him as having a disability. As a result, Ryan was treated the same as everyone else, which served him well as the years passed and he progressed both physically and emotionally.

As he grew older and his desire to participate in faster and more demanding activities became more evident, he was introduced to the world of wheelchair basketball at the age of nine. Attending a wheelchair basketball demo with his parents and being captivated by the speed and agility of the wheelchair bound athletes, he found himself convinced that this was exactly what he needed. From that point on, sports took on a whole new dimension for Ryan, as he was now able to participate in games that required speed and movement that he was previously unable to achieve. In high school he participated very competitively in tennis, a sport that without question is physically demanding. If he faced an obstacle, he would do whatever necessary to overcome it.

As impressive as he was in playing tennis, it was basketball that would ultimately dominate his focus, determination, and effort. Thus, at the age of seventeen, Ryan set a personal goal to make the U23 National Team of the National Wheelchair Basketball Association. Having written the goal on paper and having hung it above his bed, he was constantly reminded that the hard work and consistent training could one day make this goal a reality. Sacrificing time that may otherwise have been spent with high school friends, he took his workouts seriously, for he was convinced that without tremendous effort and diligence, his goal could not be met. As a result, he did indeed make the 2013 National team, followed by the USA men's team. Now playing with some of the very best basketball players in the United States, he would have to push himself even harder. Competing at the 2013 America's Cup in Bogota, Columbia, he and the USA team were now facing the most highly skilled and competitive wheelchair basketball teams that the world had to offer. Winning the America's Cup and the accompanying gold medal would be a victory that would, to Ryan, be worth all of the effort and sacrifice he had ever given. Every aspect of his driven and motivated mindset would now be demanded of him. At this time everything needed to come together perfectly for Ryan and the team as a whole if victory would become a reality; and come together it did. Ryan and his teammates not only won the gold medal, but they also experienced the incredible feeling of overcoming the very obstacles that would prevent most people from even trying. When asked about how he felt upon receiving the gold medal, Ryan happily responded, "When I won the gold medal, I couldn't wipe the smile off my face."

With his entire future before him, Ryan understands that there is more to life than winning a gold medal. Heading off to the University of Illinois, to which he's received a five year scholarship, he will be double majoring in broadcasting journalism and physical education. Though his future holds many options, whether it's a career in broadcasting journalism, teaching physical education, or competing as a paid professional basketball player, Ryan makes it very clear that it will be God who guides him into the future. Through it all, Ryan realizes that he wouldn't be where he is today without friends and family, as well as many others who have helped and influenced him in positive ways. Because of this, Ryan likewise desires to impact the lives of people whom God brings into his life, challenging and encouraging others with disabilities. Finally, when questioned concerning his participation in the 2016 Olympics in Rio, Ryan says it is indeed a big goal. Yes, it is a big goal; however, with the *supercharged* mindset of Ryan Neiswender, it may very well become a reality.

Sarah Higley

For many young people a short-term mission trip can prove to be a most challenging, convicting, and motivating time. To participate in such an activity usually proves to have a very positive influence in the lives of all involved. Often, however, when the task is completed and the individuals return home, the emotional impact of the experience slowly fades with the progression of time. The memories may remain, but the heart-felt compassion and burden for those served may be overlooked and forgotten. There are some individuals, however, who maintain that compassion, that burden which prompted them to get involved in the first place.

Sarah Higley describes herself as always having an adventurous spirit, even as a child. Never really intending to become involved in missions, but prompted by her desire for adventure, Sarah found herself participating in a church trip to a girls' orphanage in Haiti. Finding her heart broken through the trusting, tender love offered her by a young orphaned girl, she realized at that moment that she wanted to spend the rest of her life trying to help those like that little one. This was to be an experience not to be forgotten and would dramatically influence Sarah's decisions for her future.

The following summer, at the age of seventeen, still impacted by the experience in Haiti, Sarah set her sights on a trip to Africa. This trip, however, would be different, for this time she would be going alone. For over two months she would be volunteering at the

Rehoboth Children's Village in South Africa. So with a degree of uncertainty, a concern with feeling lonely, and an awkward anticipation of engaging with children in school work and other activities, Sarah nonetheless moved forward with preparations for the trip. Through the encouragement, prayers, and financial support of many, the trip, indeed, not only became a reality, but also a means by which Sarah would experience first hand the blessings and enablement of the God in whom she trusts.

Upon her arrival in South Africa at the Children's Village, which would become her home for the next several weeks, the outpouring of love and anticipation by the children was most welcoming and uplifting. Getting to know the names as well as the personalities of the fifty-five young people at the village would prove to be not only challenging, but also exhilarating. As Sarah became engaged in the daily activities of each child, she came to the full realization of the importance of her work. Not only was she meeting the physical, emotional, intellectual, and spiritual needs of the children, but she was likewise aiding in the growth and development of South Africa's future leaders.

The joy and fulfillment that Sarah was experiencing as the days and weeks progressed was further enhanced by the zeal and enthusiasm of the local church youth group. Their zeal is founded upon the overwhelming hope they have in an all-powerful God who is actively using them, as teenagers, to make a difference. Their faith and hope is a constant motivator to promote change within their community, as well as throughout their country and even throughout the world. Their desire is to be a catalyst for change, but not only in the physical, political, or economic sense. Though young, these individuals see the greatest hope in the promise that there is much more beyond this life: the promise of heaven and the rewards stored up for and awaiting them there. Thus, the change they desire within the community is a spiritual one. They realize that, above all else, the God of the Bible provides the only real hope, and that is the hope they seek to share. These young people see real needs in the lives of those around them, and they are taking action to meet those needs.

When asked what personal goals she may have had prior to leaving for Africa, Sarah clearly expressed her desire to show love to the children, be a Godly influence in their young lives, and to learn through it all whether God intended this to be her future. Reflecting upon the trip, Sarah knows without doubt that she enriched the lives of the children through the love she shared with them. But that love goes full circle, in that she experienced a tremendous joy through receiving the children's love in return.

Without doubt Sarah's love and compassion for people was enhanced through her time spent serving in Africa. She makes it very clear that the compassion she now knows is the result of the Lord's working within her heart and life. It's a compassion that will drive her future. At eighteen years of age, Sarah is currently studying to obtain an associate degree in Bible, as well as a degree in social work, all in preparation for a life on the mission field or, perhaps, social work within her own country. In speaking with Sarah Higley, one point is made very obvious, her future is not about herself, it's about others... and that's what I believe defines her as a *supercharged* teen.

www.ingramcontent.com/pod-product-compliance
Lightning Source LLC
Chambersburg PA
CBHW071903020426
42331CB00010B/2645